the Mad Keen Golfer's Road Trip

National Library of New Zealand Cataloguing-in-Publication Data

Hyde, Tom, 1947-
The Mad Keen Golfer's Road Trip : 50 trips for teeing off at
New Zealand's 161 best golf courses / by Tom Hyde.
ISBN-13: 978-1-86941-808-3
ISBN-10: 1-86941-808-5
1. Golf—New Zealand. 2. Golf courses—New Zealand. I. Title.
796.3520993—dc 22

A RANDOM HOUSE BOOK
published by
Random House New Zealand
18 Poland Road, Glenfield, Auckland, New Zealand

www.randomhouse.co.nz

First published 2006

ISBN-13: 978 1 86941 808 3
ISBN-10: 1 86941 808 5

Maps: Deborah Hinde
Cover image: Tranz/Corbis
Cover and text design: Nick Turzynski, redinc, Auckland
Printed in China by Everbest Printing Co Ltd

the Mad Keen Golfer's Road Trip

50 trips for teeing off at New Zealand's 161 best golf courses

Tom Hyde

RANDOM HOUSE
NEW ZEALAND

Here were decent godless people,
Their only monument the asphalt road
And a thousand lost golf balls.

George Eliot
The Rock, 1938

Acknowledgements

For me, to play every golf course in this book would have been possible only if the publisher was happy to wait three years for the manuscript. That's about how long it would take to play the 161 golf courses reported on here, playing one a week. But because we agreed the book should appear sooner, to say nothing of the fact that I should survive to tell the tale, I relied on the experience and knowledge of others. With that in mind, I wish to acknowledge, more or less in order of appearance, those who made this book possible. Any mistakes are entirely their fault . . . just kidding.

Don Hope, Pip King, Brendan Telfer, Peter Williams, John Lister, Kevin McGechie, Daphne Schollum, Ted McDougall, Brendan Allen, Mark Rose, Ron Corbett, David Lockwood, Mike Lee, Greg Fitzgerald, Ross Keown, Craig Owen, James Gill, Don Finlayson, Tim Wilkinson, Katerina Mataira, Marj Duncan, Dave Jones, Paul Owen, Ralph Bennett, Dave McCallum, Terry Prentice, James Marshall, Bryce Mawhinney, Brady Polkinghorn, Rex Gould, Peter Hay-McKenzie, Patrick Smith, Warren Collett, Karen Collins, Waimakariri Wyatt, Brian Jopson, Ian Litchfield, Clair McPherson, Simon Owen, Rob Sinkinson, Craig Dixon, John Harder, Bruce Archer, John Weston, Brenda Ormsby, Stan Hooper, Robbie Peterson, Franz Wetzel, Neil Kenny, Russell Williamson, Kim Southerden, Allan Shaw, Dave Moore, Kerry Brosnan, Stuart Jones, Jim Newbigin, Judy O'Rourke, Bryce Patrick, Ian Hepenstall, Peter Harrison, Colin Robertson, Mike Gainsford, Mike Stanley, Annette Laugesen, Graham Norquay, Paul Skilton, Ernie Poole, Anthony Doyle, Lynne Shaskey, Sean Higgins, Shaun Hewitt, Nigel Davis, Ernie Johnston, Mike Boshoff, Bjorn Peterson, George Morrison, Pita Austin, Bruce Paddon, Ian Cleveland, Fred Bartrum, Helen and Stuart Webster, Neville Lyons, Cushla McGillivray, Tom Ratima, Heather Greig, Ray Lash, Blair Coburn, Dennis Cheyne, Mark Whalen, Ron Fairbairn, Susan Somerville, Steve Wallace, Lance Duckett, Glenn Naylor, Jack Oliver, Dylan Lindstrom, Brad Carter, Cath Berry, Matt Casey, Darryl Coley, Neville Baldwin, Stuart Thompson, David Faulls, Georgina Greenwood, Garry Ahern, Brad Carter, Steve Wallace, Richard Woodhouse, Ken Osbourne, Glyn Delany, Jordan Dasler, Shirley Startup, Mark Millings, Lorna Clarke, Lesley Syron, Peter Bourke, Jack Hammond, Brendon Cross, Allan McKay, Brendon Wright, Doug Harradine, Margaret Mitchell, John Humphries, Andrew

Whiley, Neil Metcalfe, Scott Riordan, Euan Jamieson, Colin Conway, Kit Collins, Willie Muunu, Andrew Horan, and the old boys with a wicked sense of humour who play Monday mornings at Queens Park in Invercargill. A special thanks to Bob Schumacher and Phil Aickin who read and commented on the manuscript. Thanks also to Nicola Legat and Nic McCloy at Random House.

Publications I found helpful were *The Golfer, NZ Golf Gazette, New Zealand Golf magazine, The New Zealand Golf Guide,* and a 1971 classic by John Morris and Leonard Cobb entitled *Great Golf Holes of New Zealand.*

Useful websites included:
www.nzgolfcourses.co.nz
www.nzgolfdirectory.co.nz
www.golfstays.co.nz
www.golfnewzealand.co.nz
www.golfguide.co.nz
www.smartcars.co.nz
www.bestofgolfnewzealand.com
www.nzgolf.org.nz and
www.rentaffinity.co.nz.

Lastly, Tourism New Zealand's visitor information network, with branches in every town, was especially useful. I sometimes drove into a new town looking in the first instance for the 'i' sign, not a golf course.

All of the green fees quoted in this book were correct at time of printing.

Contents

Foreword

This book is for men and women, young and old, who are so mad-keen about golf they can't get enough of it playing just once on a normal weekend, so at least once a year they need to plan their own long weekend on the road to work off that burning desire and visit new places.

Because these trips are conceived as three-day trips, playing a different course each day, the logic of the road meant that some very fine country golf courses, such as Taumarunui and Balclutha, missed the cut. Courses were selected as much for where they are as for what they are.

All the courses identified in this book are 18 holes. As heartless as it is, 9-hole courses and funky little tracks like the 10-hole golf course on Waiheke Island and the 6-hole one on Stewart Island have been excluded — independent of the fact that to play the latter two you have to travel by boat.

My suggestions on where to stay and eat are only that. My view is if golfers want to stay in a camp ground or a six-star lodge that's up to them. They should do some homework of their own to find out what's best for them.

Symbols used in the text are intentionally brief. OB is for Out of Bounds, GF is for green fees, AFF represents the green fee for players affiliated to the New Zealand Golf Association, NON is the green fee for the great unwashed.

All of the courses here have changing rooms and shower facilities and a snack bar if not a café or restaurant. Most hire out golf clubs of some description, although I find it hard to see how someone could be truly mad-keen if they didn't BTO (bring their own).

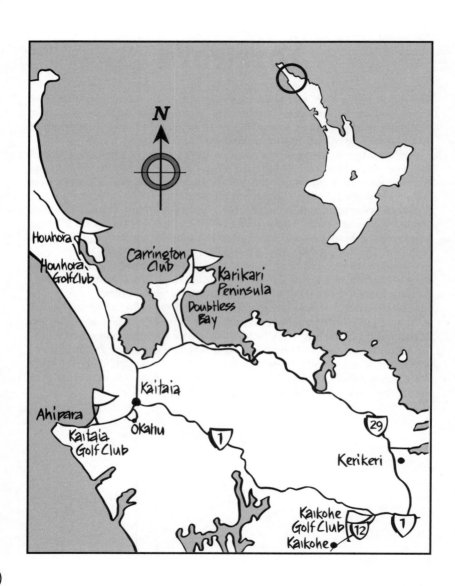

the Far North

The Far North is Cape Reinga and Cape Maria van Diemen and Kupe arriving in a waka. It's Spirits Bay, giant sand dunes, and the extraordinary Ninety Mile Beach, even if it's not exactly 90 miles long. It's an ancient kauri forest with at least two stellar attractions, Tane Mahuta and Te Matua Ngahere.

On your way to the Far North on State Highway 1 turn right onto State Highway 12 to Kaikohe, the original home of the great Ngapuhi chief, Hone Heke Pokai. It was near here on Lake Omapere that he built Te Kahika, an impregnable pa that the British tried twice unsuccessfully to invade. If it's European artefacts you're looking for then take note: Kaikohe has on public display the largest plough ever made in New Zealand.

The **Kaikohe Golf Club** is on the corner of State Highway 12 and Ngawha Springs Road. If you choose to have a hot soak and stay the night, try the Ngawha Springs Motel. The Jailer's Rest café in town serves good coffee.

The golf course at Kaikohe keeps its greens in excellent condition all year round and because the course is only 5400 metres long from the white tees and 4800 metres long from the yellow tees, it's user-friendly too. It has only three bunkers (sand traps) and two of them you can deal with at once — at the attractive par-3 5th hole.

Only one of the two ponds on the course comes into play, at the par-3 16th hole, where the water is closer to the tee than the green. To hit your ball into the water really means that you've 'topped' or 'domed' your tee shot, something mad-keen golfers rarely do. Still, players somehow manage to do it. Club member Willie Muunu told me, 'Everyone here has done it. It's a mental thing.'

Or maybe there's a dark story to this pond I failed to uncover?

Beware the drain cutting across the fairway at the par-4 7th hole and if you can drive the ball long off the tee, you'll love the par-5 8th hole here because it's possible for big hitters to reach the green in two. The club played host in 2006 to the Northland Amateur Stroke play championship. GF: $20 for all.

Drive on through the Mangamuku Gorge and with luck you won't get stuck behind a truck. Kaitaia is less than an hour away. The **Kaitaia Golf Club** is a classic seaside links that is actually located in Ahipara, a small settlement 14 kilometres from town on Ninety Mile Beach. You're on the right road if you drive by Okahu Estate, the northernmost winery in New Zealand.

The Bay Links Lodge Motel in Ahipara is so close to the golf course you could hit the clubhouse with a 7-iron — not that I'm suggesting you try. The Bay Links has seven clean, self-contained units. I note that because players wishing to play and stay the night by the sea are advised to stock up at a Kaitaia supermarket before driving out for the night. Alternatively, Kaitaia has a selection of motels to choose from, although The Beachcomber is the only noteworthy restaurant (in my view) in town.

The golf course is long or not, depending on the wind. The par-3 6th hole, for example, is not long; it's only 114 metres from the white tees. But it plays from a tee box that's the highest elevated (read: most exposed) on the course.

The club should build a viewing stand up there, for it would be great fun to watch players tee off into the prevailing wind. To reach the green on a quiet day this hole calls for little more than a short-iron for both men and women. But when the wind is stirred up it's like some kind of devil, for reaching the green, believe it or not, can mean pulling a fairway wood out of the bag.

The rough here is truly rough and it's not something that simply borders the fairway as punishment for a stray shot. Here there are no 'fairways' as such, only mowed grass and patches of sand and cut coastal strips shaped by the long, slow movement of dunes over time. This scratchiness combines with a series of bunkers (as if the course didn't have enough sand already) to make Kaitaia tricky and tons of fun at the same time. Tip: Learning the technique for making good ball-contact when the ball is either above or below your feet comes in handy here, for if there is any dead flat ground I didn't see it.

The greens are in good nick. Norfolk pines and clumps of pohutukawa accentuate the landscape. The sound of the sea is a wonderful constant. The 18th hole could be called the 'signature', for it plays directly towards one of Ahipara's signatures: Mt Whangatauatia. GF: $25 for all.

If it rains, visit the Ancient Kauri Kingdom just north of town. It's a New Zealand Tourism prize-winning outpost and, who knows, you may feel inspired to buy a finely crafted set of kauri table and chairs for $10,000. The next day, drive down State Highway 10 for 20 minutes to the turn off onto the Karikari

Peninsula and the **Carrington Club**. Check in at either the resort's villas or lodge rooms. The Villa and Golf Option is a package that includes accommodation, golf, breakfast, and access to the heated swimming pool, the spa, and the tennis courts.

The golf course at Carrington, with its spectacular views of Doubtless Bay, was designed by American Matt Dye. It opened in December 2003 as part of a full-service resort that includes a lodge, a vineyard and winery, a 3000-acre Black Angus stud farm, and a secluded white-sand beach. A resident instructor can introduce you to skeet and trap shooting (clay pigeons) if you're still feeling aggressive after golf. For a quiet retreat try the library or the billiard room.

On the golf course, the 15th tee at the top of the hill affords panoramic views of the coast, although the signature hole is probably the beautiful and deadly par-3 7th hole that plays over a small lake back toward the lodge.

Carrington is not a links: it's a hilly parklands-style course. With that in mind, hiring a cart will make getting around easier . . . and let's face it you're on holiday, no? Maori totems carved by Hector Busby and natural wetlands enhance the Far North look and feel of the course. GF: Overnight guests $85, $85 AFF, $135 NON. The Carrington Club is not exclusive, local residents play here too. It's casual and relaxed. If it rains head up the hill to Karikari Estate winery for lunch followed by an afternoon appointment at the spa. Alternatively, drive down State Highway 10 for 20 minutes to the Mangonui Fish Shop for the best fish and chips in New Zealand.

Kaikohe Golf Club
Phone 09 401 0815
Email kaikohe@golf.co.nz

Kaitaia Golf Club
Web www.ahipara.co.nz/kgc
Phone 09 409 4833
Email kaitaia@golf.co.nz

Carrington Club
Web www.carrington.co.nz
Phone 09 408 7222
Email info@carrington.co.nz

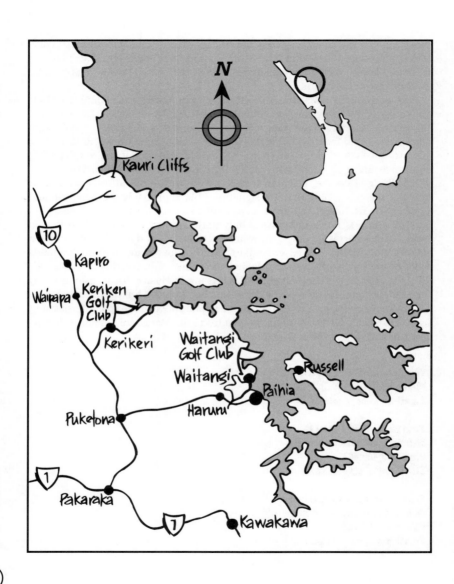

the Bay of Islands

The Bay of Islands, as Captain James Cook named it in 1769, was always a hive of human activity. Maori tribes congregated here in pre-European times at Kororareka, a small settlement that became a whaling port (and the so-called 'hellhole of the Pacific') before it was ransacked by Hone Heke in 1845 and renamed Russell.

Today, as one of the country's premier holiday destinations, it remains a busy port-of-call for just about everything from deep-sea fishing and sailing to golf. The **Kerikeri Golf Club** is easy enough to find because it's on Fairway Road which runs off the main street, Kerikeri Road, through town. You'll know you've found the course when you drive across a one-lane wooden bridge.

This course is one of the prettiest in the country, as it's beautifully maintained and shaped by native trees and bush, and planted out in a way that makes it feel like someone's private garden estate. The course is one of the few in New Zealand with couch grass fairways that make playing here like playing on a smooth green carpet. Of course, that only makes the rough feel rougher.

With the rare exception, the holes on this course play straight up and back among tree-lined and bush-clad fairways. The best hole on any golf course, in my view, is often not the Number 1 stroke hole. Such is the case here, where the par-3 13th may be only 100 metres from the white tees but it's virtually a straight drop down, from an elevated tee to a green flanked by two ponds and three bunkers.

It looks easy enough until you come up short and watch your ball disappear into the drink or come to rest all covered in sand. Some players try to avoid the hazards here by going long, in which case they risk running off the sudden shoulder at the back of the green. This hole is, in fact, the Number 18 stroke hole, the 'easiest' hole on the course. But no hole in golf is ever as benign as the scorecard suggests. GF: $35 AFF, $45 NON.

Either before or after your round of golf here, you'll need to settle on accommodation. The Bay of Islands, with Kerikeri, Paihia, and Russell so close together, means the options are many and varied. A quick on-line search will show you what I mean. Barring that, the Cottle Court Motel is directly across Kerikeri Road from the golf course. The string of Kerikeri shops, cafés, and licensed restaurants are right next door. And as you might expect from a busy tourist hub, Kerikeri has a veritable menu of places to eat, from inexpensive ethnic takeaways to fine dining.

The next morning drive up State Highway 10 for 15 minutes and you'll see the sign on the right-hand side of the road pointing the way to fabulous **Kauri Cliffs**. Since it opened in 2000, Kauri Cliffs has established itself as one of the best golf courses and small luxury resorts in the world. Here you can either choose to stay overnight and leave the real world behind completely, or you can just pay green fees and play this extraordinary cliff-top course, possibly the best course in New Zealand, on a day visit.

The course, designed by David Harmon of Orlando, Florida, has couch grass fairways and some of the finest greens you'll ever play, even if they will at first seem especially fast. The course as a whole is as eye-popping as any golf course anywhere because of its location on (above) the coast.

Six of the holes on the back nine play along the edge of cliffs with panoramic ocean views to the Cavalli Islands and beyond. Tip: Do not wander too close to the edge in search of a stray golf ball. Here 15 holes have extraordinary views. Most visitors will enjoy the course most when there is little or no wind, yet even in a steady breeze this course is truly a 'must play before you die'.

If you do decide to spend at least one night here, you'll receive a 10 per cent reduction on green fees.

Overnight stays range from $500 to $6500 depending on the type of accommodation and the season. All rates include pre-dinner drinks, a sumptuous à la carte meal, and breakfast the next morning. Men are asked to wear a jacket for dinner. GF: $180 AFF, $300 NON May–September; $225 AFF $400 NON October–April.

The **Waitangi Golf Club** is just a short drive back south on State Highway 10. It's also quite spectacular for its panoramic coastal views, only the outlook here is not over a dramatic cliff-framed coastline, it's out over stunning blue bays, shimmering harbours and emerald isles.

The 10th to the 15th holes on this golf course are especially exhilarating for the views and quite often for the golf, too! They play on the seaward side of a paved road that winds its way through the course. The par-4 11th hole is a terrific walk that sweeps down and around to the left and toward the bay. The par-3 12th and the par-5 13th play back up to the road before the par-4 14th bends around a gully and back down toward the sea again, where the green is nestled inside a grove of pohutukawa that on the day of my visit were in full bloom. It was 'wow' all the way.

Waitangi is hilly in parts but it's a wonderful wide-open course that's not a difficult walk. Like the course at Kerikeri, Waitangi too is renewing itself with couch grass fairways. The club hires out Callaway golf clubs, second-hand ones originally from Kauri Cliffs. Say 'g'day' to Alex. GF: $35 AFF, $45 NON.

There's a Copthorne Hotel conveniently located at the bottom of the road from the golf course and within walking distance of the restaurants and bars of Paihia. If it rains join an Embrace Waitangi guided tour or contact Taiamai Tours (www.taiamaitours.co.nz) for a heritage tour in a traditional Maori waka.

Kerikeri Golf Club
Web www.nzgolfcourses.co.nz/kerikeri
Phone 09 407 8776
Email kerikerigolf@xtra.co.nz

Kauri Cliffs
Web www.kauricliffs.com
Phone 09 407 0010
Email proshop@kauricliffs.com

Waitangi Golf Club
Web www.waitangigolf.co.nz
Phone 09 402 7713
Email waitangi@golf.co.nz

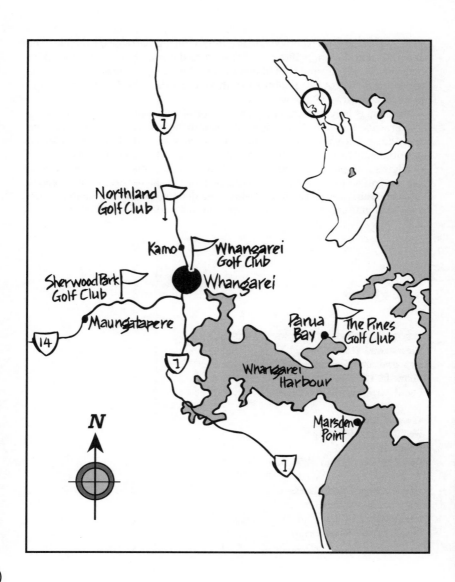

Whangarei

If there is a singular development in Whangarei in recent times that makes this stop worthwhile for the non-golfer it's the Town Basin, a waterfront district of shops and cafés that nicely complements the marina. If time is on your side, you may want to take a peak inside Clapham's Clock Museum and if you're uncertain about where to stay, the Kingsgate Hotel, with a restaurant, gym, and swimming pool, is located on Riverside Drive opposite the marina. For a quieter overnight abode swing right at the marina up Hatea Drive to Pembroke Motor Lodge.

Whangarei is blessed with *four* decent 18-hole golf courses. Assuming you're there to play three of them in three days, it's up to you which one doesn't make the cut. But if I were in charge of the tour we'd play all four, taking four days if necessary, and start with the bucolic **Sherwood Park Golf Club** 10 minutes out on State Highway 14 or what's known locally as 'the road to Dargaville'.

That there's an equestrian track across the road from the golf course is perfectly fitting, because the landscape here, apart from new homes, is a scene from Gainsborough. It's pretty, it's rustic, or is it simply the enchanting stone walls that are, golfers take note, Out of Bounds? The par-4 2nd hole is bounded on the right by a stone wall that is so enchanting it can attract a golf ball, if you're not careful.

The long (379 metres from the white tees) par-4 13th followed by the par-3 14th are quietly spoken of as 'Amen Corner'. The 13th may be long but the 14th can prove to be like Jaws. Just when you think you're going along swimmingly, either the pond to the left of the green or the (gorgeous) puriri tree at the front right gets you.

When some of the country's top club players gathered here in 2002 for the National Interprovincial Championship they found a course that's relatively flat, defined by groves of trees and clumps of bush, but with fairways that bend and break off in surprising ways. Sherwood Park is not long, in fact big hitters can leave their driver in the bag most of the way. But it does demand solid, smart targeted golf shots. The greens were in very good condition. GF: $25 AFF, $40 NON.

On your way back into town, stop at the Whangarei Museum and Heritage Park. You'll have driven by it on your way out to the golf course. The Kiwi House here is the home of a North Island brown kiwi named Kakama. The old steam engines out the back are pretty cool, too.

The next morning follow State Highway 1 north through Whangarei to Kamo. Through Kamo, turn left onto Pipiwai Road where you'll find the **Northland Golf Club**, a lovely country course close to the city that, with its host of native trees and bird life, is like playing golf in a scenic reserve. Here, wood pigeons share a peaceful co-existence with flying golf balls.

The course is slightly hilly but its slopes and a stream that cuts through it add to its character. Water comes into play on six holes including the Number 1 stroke hole, the par-4 5th — a long dogleg right. Recently the club built a new green closer to the stream at the par-4 11th hole but, as if to keep things fair, the stream at the par-3 16th has been diverted. Still, this picturesque hole plays across a valley to a green that, like all greens here, has been recently upgraded. In keeping with that upgrade, Northland also installed a new drainage system making it playable even on the wettest days in winter — if you're also a mad-keen duck. GF: $20 AFF, $30 NON.

From the Town Basin follow Hatea Drive to the top of the hill. Turn right at Denby Crescent for the **Whangarei Golf Club**, home of the famous 'split pine' on the par-4 6th hole. The tree hasn't been the same since it was struck by lightning. Now it looks like a warped rugby goalpost, seductive in its own way as it invites you to play a shot between the 'uprights' — even if it's not the best way to play the hole. The tree is to the right of the fairway so if you wish to play through it, just for fun, it takes a well-placed duck-hook to keep the ball in play.

As if the competition in Whangarei is driving the golf clubs to, well, lift their game, six of the holes on the back nine here were recently renovated. The course looks and feels similar to the Northland Golf Club, only the landscape is flatter and if there are any wood pigeons here I didn't see them. Apart from the famous tree on the 6th hole, if there's a 'signature' here it might be the par-3 15th that plays across a small lake. Another pond waits at the elbow of the par-5 10th hole, a dogleg right around the water. GF: $30 AFF, $40 NON.

The Pines Golf Club is a scenic little course on the shores of Parua Bay. From the white tees it's the shortest of the four courses on this trip. Follow Riverside Drive out toward the airport, only turn left onto Whangarei Heads Road. The course plays along the flat and up across ridges with elevated views of the bay, especially at the par-4 7th hole.

A stream cuts through the course making the front nine as interesting as the back, especially at the short par-4 4th with *two* creeks cutting across the fairway and a puriri tree proudly poised directly in front of the green.

The par-5 10th hole plays directly toward the bay and here the course, parklands in every other way, feels more like a links. The par-4 11th and the par-5 12th holes play along the shoreline of Parua Bay.

Don't let the grumpy manager put you off. GF: $20 AFF, $25 NON.

Sherwood Park Golf Club
Web www.sherwoodpark.nzgolf.net
Phone 09 434 6900
Email sherwood@golf.co.nz

Northland Golf Club
Web www.northland.nzgolf.net
Phone 09 435 0042
Email northland.club@golf.co.nz

Whangarei Golf Club
Web www.nzgolfcourses.co.nz/whangarei
Phone 09 437 0775
Email mtdenby@paradise.net.nz

The Pines Golf Club
Phone 09 436 2246
Email the.pines@golf.co.nz

Whangarei

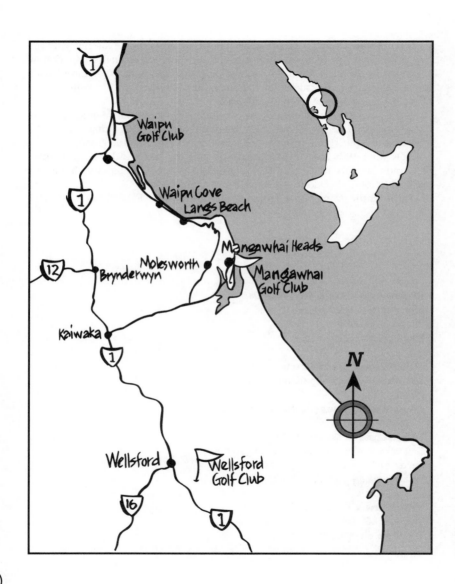

Northland

Northland's east coast between Auckland and Whangarei is a series of some of the best beaches and bays in the country, so it's not surprising that it's a popular region for long weekend escapes. Here visitors can engage in a host of outdoor activities from fishing and sailing to diving and coastal horse-trekking.

Tucked in amongst all the seaside fun, however, are three fine golf courses that deserve more attention than they usually get. The **Mangawhai Golf Club** is a two-hour drive from Auckland. Look for the turn-off on State Highway 1 at Kaiwaka. The town of Mangawhai was once a sleepy coastal village but it's come alive, thanks mainly to the high demand for coastal real estate. Go on-line to www.mangawhai.org.nz and you'll see what I mean.

The golf course is located on the north side of town off Molesworth Drive or what is the main road through to Waipu. If you're still undecided where to stay while you're there, an information kiosk is conveniently located next to the drive into the golf course parking lot. As the name suggests, the Fairways Bed & Breakfast is directly opposite the course but then you may prefer driving, if only to stay somewhere with sea views.

Mangawhai is not a links course. Ted McDougall, the popular professional here, compares this golf course to the English country courses he played in the 1950s and '60s as a top amateur and touring professional. In that way the course is, ironically, something of a relief from the intensity of all the seaside activity.

The layout of this attractive course, with the location of trees and native bush, means that each hole here is separated from the others in a way that enhances your sense of privacy. Hit a bad shot and it's likely no one but your playing partners will notice. The course is slightly hilly, but it's not a difficult walk and with few bunkers and little water its possible here for the average player to be better-than-average providing they keep the ball in the fairway. The fairways here are generously wide but depending on how long the grass is on the day, the rough at Mangawhai can be truly rough.

The 1st and 18th holes are very good opening and closing holes for the casual player because they are relative short par-5s that can leave you feeling good about yourself at the start and at the finish of your round. The 1st is straight down a flat fairway to a mid-size green with only a small grassy knoll on the front left to stop a ball from rolling to the pin. The 18th is a rolling fairway with bunkers on the left and right that plays up to an elevated green.

If there's a signature hole here, however, it might be the par-4 7th simply because it features the most unique green on the course. The green sits up above two deep bunkers front left and right and it's rimmed by a grassy ridge that gives it the appearance of resting in a bowl. Because the club has one of the best websites of all the courses identified in this book, you can see it for yourself on-line. GF: $30 AFF, $35 NON midweek; $40 AFF, $45 NON weekends.

For dinner after your round try either the Barracuda Café or the Sail Rock Café in the shopping centre at the bottom of the hill from the golf club. The next day follow the coast road over to Waipu. The road winds across a ridge into Bream Bay and through Langs Beach and Waipu Cove before it swings around into Waipu. Turn right back out to State Highway 1 and head north for two minutes and you'll see the entrance to the **Waipu Golf Club** on your right.

Waipu is a terrific links course built on sandy soil and with all the trappings that come with seaside golf. It's the site of the popular Bream Bay Classic, a pro-am event once won by New Zealand professional Marcus Wheelhouse who, along with three others, holds the course record of 67.

The club has taken out many of the pines that once shaped its fairways, so it's more exposed today than ever to Bream Bay in a way that makes it especially testing when the wind blows. But wind or not, it's one of the most scenic courses in Northland. The fairways can be scruffy (this is a links course, after all) but the greens are kept in good condition all year round.

One of the best holes on the front nine is the par-5 8th hole that sweeps around towards the sea. It can be equally exhilarating and frustrating to play, depending on the prevailing wind. On the back nine the par-4 12th is not long but it's a dogleg right that also plays toward the sea. GF: $30 AFF, $35 NON.

If your accommodation in Mangawhai is not up to scratch, try the more luxurious Royal Palm Lodge in Waipu for comfort, fine dining, and great sea views. But assuming it's summer and you are driving back to Mangawhai for the night, stop at Waipu Cove or Langs Beach, two of the best beaches in Northland, for a swim.

The next day drive back out to State Highway 1 to Kaiwaka and make the short drive south to the **Wellsford Golf Club**, an attractive country course just south of the town centre. The course is always in good nick. It has small greens, only a few innocuous bunkers, and no water hazards, and though it's hilly, it's not a course that's difficult to walk and to score well on. Because it's the final course on your long weekend of golf in Northland, it should send you home feeling good about your game.

Wellsford is only 5100 metres long off the white tees, but the hilly nature of the course, and its elevated greens with some requiring 'blind' approach shots, means that to score well the short game is more important than the long game. Good touch around the greens and the ability to get up-and-down with a short pitch shot are very useful skills to have here.

That said, big hitters will have fun at the monster par-5 4th hole, the longest hole on the course. But don't get so caught up in your splendid 250-metre drive here that you wind up in the line of fire from players teeing off on the par-3 15th that plays across the fairway of the 4th. If no one is around to collect your green fees, use the honesty box! GF: $25 AFF, $30 NON.

Mangawhai Golf Club
Web www.mangawhaigolf.co.nz
Phone 09 431 4807
Email mangawhai@paradise.net.nz

Waipu Golf Club
Web www.waipugolfclub.org.nz
Phone 09 432 0259
Email info@waipugolfclub.org.nz

Wellsford Golf Club
Web www.wellsford.nzgolf.net
Phone 09 423 8385
Email wgc@wellsford.co.nz

Ted McDougall
See **Local Heroes,** *page 211*

Northland

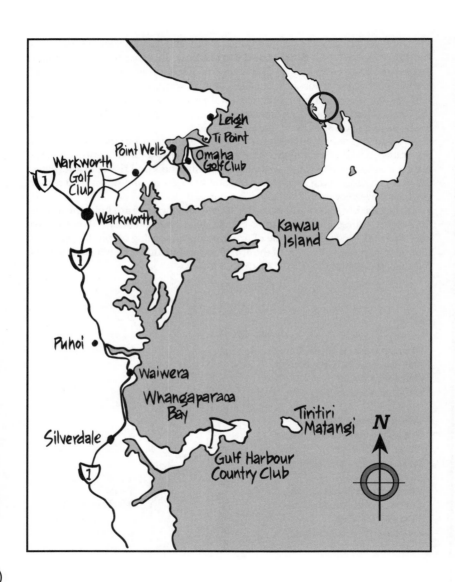

the Kowhai Coast

With the new northern motorway extension, Warkworth is now less than an hour's drive from Auckland, a fact that goes a long way towards explaining how this former farming district came to be carved up into 'lifestyle' blocks and vineyards. Warkworth now boasts six wineries and a variety of arts and crafts galleries and shops that have altogether made the 'Kowhai Coast', as this region is sometimes called for the yellow-flowered kowhai trees, an especially attractive place to visit over a long weekend — golf or no golf.

As you come into town on State Highway 1 turn right at the second set of traffic lights and follow the sign to Omaha. About three kilometres further along that road you'll see the turn-off on your right to the **Warkworth Golf Club**. The club has a new clubhouse and, in an effort to attract more members and guests, this gently rolling, attractive country course has recently undertaken some successful landscaping that has further enhanced its reputation as the 'best kept secret of the North' (as the club calls itself). But the increased popularity of this golf course means that booking a tee time is necessary.

This 5360-metre course is not long, but it's hilly. The par-4 2nd hole, for example, is less than 300 metres long from the white tees but it plays (ugh!) uphill. The par-4 3rd (the Number 1 stroke hole) plays back down the hill and, as if its severely sloping fairway — a dogleg right that falls off sharply to the right — were still too easy, the approach shot is around the corner and back up yet another hill to a plateau green. Come up short and your ball trickles back into the gully. Oh, joy!

Warkworth is a collection of odd-holes, ones you'll never find on any other golf course in the country. The oddest of them all is the short par-4 5th that plays from an elevated tee down a hill and around a grove of pine and macrocarpa. But because the trees are actually below the tee, the unavoidable temptation (for men) is to drive the ball *over* the trees, straight at the green. Wimps, on the other hand, play it more conventionally by hitting a mid-iron to the elbow in position for an easy short-iron to the green. The course has five short par-5s that can make even high handicappers feel good about themselves. Come to think of it, maybe that's why this course has become so popular in recent years. GF: $25 AFF, $30 NON.

After playing at Warkworth drive further along the road to Omaha (and Leigh) until you come to the sign pointing right to Snells Beach. Check in there at the Salty Dog Inn, a clean and comfortable motel with special stay-and-play golf packages for Warkworth and Omaha Beach. The **Omaha Beach Golf Club** where you'll play the next day is only a short, scenic drive away.

You'll know you're close to the golf course when you come upon a causeway over an inlet of the Whangateau Harbour. You'll see the golf course on the right. Omaha Beach is a links course, though the first three holes are more parklands-style as they were part of the original course when it was only nine holes. Extraordinarily for a small club, Omaha hired John Darby & Associates, better known for their work at Millbrook and Clearwater resorts in the South Island, to create a new nine holes and make it into a true links course. The fun they designed begins across the road at the par-4 4th and continues right through to the par-3 12th when the course crosses back over the road and links (sorry) again with the original course.

The par-3 8th hole here is my personal favourite. It plays over a natural wetlands to an elevated, rolling green flanked by white-sand bunkers, all with a dense grove of native trees for a backdrop. A boardwalk leads to the 9th tee. The picturesque par-3 12th requires a solid shot over a small lake to reach an elevated, sloping green with bunkers front and back. It's only the Number 14 stroke hole but it plays more difficult than that. Or is it me? GF: $30 AFF, $40 NON weekends; $24 AFF, $35 NON midweek.

Drive south on State Highway 1, turn left at Silverdale and follow the signs to the tip of the Whangaparaoa Peninsula and the **Gulf Harbour Country Club**, one of the finest resort courses in the country. Gulf Harbour is the site of the New Zealand Open, one of the two major professional tournaments in the country each year.

The club has three stay-and-play packages in association with the Gulf Harbour Lodge at the marina, a short walk from the golf course. The course is long and hilly in parts, so carts ($20) are recommended for slower players.

The front nine plays through new housing, houses owned by brave souls who have settled within range of flying golf balls. The par-5 2nd hole is one of the best par-5s in the country, long and up and around and down and back up, with bunkers protecting a 'blind' green. Still, I witnessed radio host Murray Deaker birdie it on one occasion.

The back nine at Gulf Harbour sweeps out from the clubhouse to the cliffs and panoramic sea views. After playing the par-4 12th hole, a short par-4 that plays down a steep gully and back up a steep incline to a blind green (big hitters can drive this green), stop a moment at the back of the green and take in the compelling view down the Rangitoto Channel to Auckland. There's a bench to sit on if you need it.

The 15th, 16th, and 17th holes here are possibly the most stunning trio of holes on any golf course in New Zealand. They play along the edge of the cliff where on some days the only compensation for a bad shot is the expansive view of the Hauraki Gulf.

This is the only golf course in New Zealand designed by the famed American architect, Robert Trent Jones Jr. The club has an excellent pro shop, a swimming pool, squash courts, and if it rains you can try your luck at billiards. The club has a café and restaurant or you can try the Nautilus Restaurant & Bar on the waterfront next to the lodge. GF: $85 AFF, $105 NON.

Warkworth Golf Club
Web www.warkworth.nzgolf.net
Phone 09 425 8248
Email warkworth@golf.co.nz

Omaha Beach Golf Club
Web www.nzgolfcourses.co.nz/omaha
Phone 09 422 7551
Email omaha@nzgolfcourses.co.nz

Gulf Harbour Country Club
Web www.gulfharbourcountryclub.co.nz
Phone 09 428 1380
Email proshop@gulfharbourcountryclub.co.nz

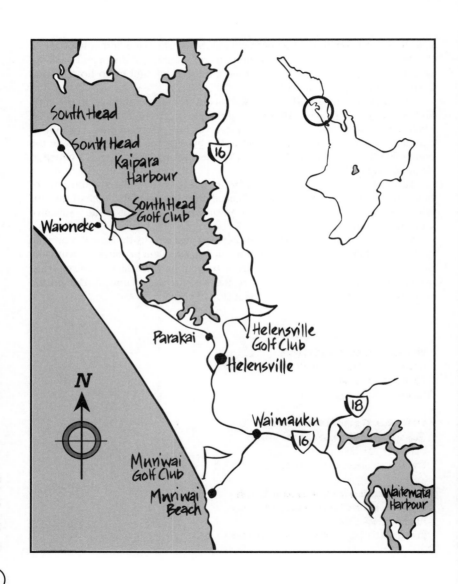

Harbour & Surf

When the Scot John McLeod, of the famous McLeod family who migrated to New Zealand from Nova Scotia, built a new kauri home in 1862, he named it after his wife Helen. He called the place Helen's Villa and in time the home and the growing settlement it was part of became known as Helensville.

From Auckland the drive out on the northwest motorway (State Highway 16) past the orchards and vineyards of Kumeu and Waimauku to Helensville takes about 50 minutes. Helensville, on the Kaipara River and only a few minutes' drive from the extraordinary Kaipara Harbour, once made its money from kauri, then dairy farming, and since the dairy factory closed, tourism. The website www.helensville.co.nz lists options for accommodation, including the classic Grand Hotel in town.

From there it's only 20 minutes out along South Head Road to the **South Head Golf Club**, a popular course because it's an easy drive yet far from the madding crowd, and the sandy hills it's built on make it playable all year round. South Head is forever in good nick; it's not expensive to play by Auckland standards, and it includes great views of the Kaipara Harbour from the back nine, especially from the 14th green that completes a short but demanding little dogleg right to the green.

Water hazards, ponds and a small lake, come into play on three holes. The 2nd and the 10th, both par-3s, play over water and should you pull your approach shot to the green at the par-5 9th too far left, that could wind up wet as well. South Head is only medium-length (5600 metres long from the white tees) but it's hilly, and on days when the wind comes in off the harbour getting up-and-down here, literally, can be more difficult than its length suggests. Tiger Woods caddied for Steve Williams here. GF: $25 midweek, $35 weekends for all.

Depending on the weather you may feel like a hot soak (or a cool swim) after your round at Parakai as you make your way back into Helensville. The Aquatic Park with hot springs is open all year round, even on Christmas Day,

Harbour & Surf

but during the winter months, after a day tramping about on the golf course, a hot soak is enough to make you forget your score. Try Black Pete's Back Alley Bar & Grill across the road for some good down-home country tucker. Alternatively, try The Kaipara, a restaurant and sports bar in Helensville.

The next day drive out on Peak Road a few minutes to the **Helensville Golf Club**. The club recently undertook some major landscaping, adding a small lake to what is already a tight, tree-lined course that's equally as popular as South Head with Auckland city golfers looking for a day in the country.

This quirky course is long and tight with small greens, so for the average player it's a surprisingly difficult course to score well on. Take the par-4 1st hole, for instance. There's no bunker, no water hazard, and it's relatively straight. But it's tree-lined and reasonably tight and it plays long, over a ridge and down to a small green that's tucked left of a grove of pine trees. Par here is a good score. No doubt some young gun has scored a birdie here, but it's hard to imagine.

Or take the par-3 3rd hole that plays over a pond and to a green, with the large and rather invasive pine tree on the left hanging out over what would normally be the most direct angle to the green. I'm surprised some club vigilantes haven't snuck out there one night and cut it down. So, you either be strong and go over the top or play out to the right, where more players than not wind up short and to the right of the green.

To par the straight, no-nonsense par-5 16th hole means clearing a gully and a bunker with your third shot. It's not a difficult hole; in fact, it's a bit of a set-up because you walk off that green with your chest out only to confront the par-4 17th that will surely make a fool of you. This short par-4 is so narrow big hitters will use an iron off the tee then follow that up with another iron to the green. The rest of us, using a driver or fairway wood, tend to either pull our tee shot left into a cow paddock or push it too far right into trees. The people here are friendly enough — it's only the course that's deceptively nasty. GF: $27 AFF, $32 NON midweek; $32 AFF, $37 NON weekends.

Drive south on State Highway 16 from Helensville to Waimauku where you'll turn right and follow the signs to Muriwai Beach. On-line: www.muriwai.com lists options for accommodation and meals. The Muriwai Beach Lodge has a restaurant and terrific views of the coast. It also overlooks the **Muriwai Beach Golf Club**, one of the best links courses in the country.

The imperious Tasman Sea forced the club to close the original front nine and build an entire new nine holes further away from the beach. The new holes have only recently settled down but among them I would choose the par-5 6th and the par-3 8th as my personal favourites. The 6th is not a dogleg so much as a banana. It sweeps around a dune that blocks any direct view of the green to this hole. It is one of the rare par-5s with a 'blind' second shot that must be placed just right to set up a third, short-iron approach to the green. The par-3 8th is not long but it plays directly into the teeth of a westerly.

The back nine at Muriwai has some of the original holes but two of the new layouts here are especially noteworthy: the par-5 12th is one of the best par-5s in the Auckland region. It bends around a bunker to the left and plays through a series of six more perfectly placed fairway and greenside bunkers to a green that, for big hitters, can be reached in two *if* they are willing to take on the sand traps.

The par-4 16th plays over a rise and down to a long, slender green set into a hillside on the left and guarded on the front by a deep black-sand bunker. Did I say the green falls off sharply on the left?

This course is especially golden in the late afternoon as the sun sets on the western horizon. GF: $30 AFF, $40 NON.

South Head Golf Club
Web www.southhead.nzgolf.net
Phone 09 420 2838
Email southhead@golf.co.nz

Helensville Golf Club
Web www.helensville.nzgolf.net
Phone 09 420 5454
Email helensville@golf.co.nz

Muriwai Beach Golf Club
Web www.muriwai.nzgolf.net
Phone 09 411 8454
Email muriwai@golf.co.nz

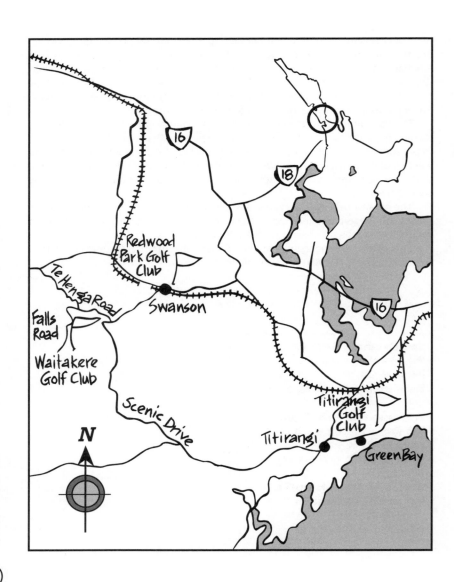

Waitakere Bush

This trip should be based from accommodation on the west coast at a place like Piha or Karekare, but for better or worse accommodation in these hideaway spots is limited to boutique one-room cottages and places that feel more like someone's home, not a place for mad-keen golfers to let their hair down. For that, try the Dalma Court Motor Inn on Great North Road in Henderson. It has 30 self-contained units and it's close to the West City shopping centre, where there's a multiplex cinema should it rain.

Find your way to the roundabout at the intersection of Great North Road and Don Buck Road and swing around onto the road to Swanson. The first street on your right past the Swanson train station will lead you to the **Redwood Park Golf Club**, a peaceful course that plays across the foothills of the Waitakere Ranges.

Redwood Park is not a long course but the fairways drop and bend and rise up in a way that makes local knowledge of the lay of the land — and consistently good shot-making to boot — necessary to score well.

The par-4 1st hole establishes the mood. It's not long, but it plays slightly uphill before it breaks sharply around to the left around hungry bunkers to a green that can only be reached by playing it straight. Big egos attempting to drive the green over the corner will only wind up in trees. Redwood Park is a modest course that doesn't like players trying to be smart.

A pond/water hazard comes into play at the new par-3 10th hole. The par-4 17th, one of the most difficult holes on the course, is a long par-4 that begins with a 'blind' tee shot down the hill to a dogleg right back up to an elevated, two-tiered green. Now, let's see someone play cute with that one.

Redwood Park is one of the most popular courses in Auckland, thus the duty secretary made it clear to me in no uncertain terms: tee times *must* be booked! And it's members-only on Saturdays! Okay, fine, this is still a great place to begin a golf trip in the 'wild west'. GF: $35 midweek, $40 weekends for all.

The next day, drive further out on Scenic Drive to Te Henga Road. Swing right to find the **Waitakere Golf Club**, one of the smallest yet most, well, scenic golf courses in the Auckland region. In contrast to Redwood Park, the folks here are more than happy to find a tee time for visitors, even on Saturday.

As its name suggests, the course sits in the middle of the Waitakere Ranges. Here the most common expression to describe the course is 'bush-clad' and for a good reason. Everything here, from the golf course to the local primary school, is clad in bush! Bush that softens the cut and thrust of the mountains and makes this hilly course feel more remote than it is.

Of course it's hilly, but not extremely so. And though it has its fair share of trees it's also relatively open and forgiving in a way that should make even high handicappers feel like, well, how about Frank Nobilo?

Nobilo, one of New Zealand's most successful touring professionals, a winner on the US PGA Tour and now a television commentator in the US, began playing here as a teenager. There's a photo on the wall of the clubhouse of young Frank as a member of the club's 1976 senior pennants team.

The tee of the short par-3 6th hole here is set back in, surprise, surprise: bush. But it's a cool place to clean your ball on a hot day and it makes the tee shot, out through a gap in all the green, quite unique. The par-3 17th hole is especially picturesque because it plays over a small lake to a sloping green.

Waitakere has only six bunkers; but it's not the bunkers that order play here so much as the hills, for playing up-and-down is decidedly different and calls for different shots than playing on the flat up-and-back. This is not an easy walking course and the club does not hire carts, so look at it this way: you're on holiday, you've got time, and playing here is like a fun trek through, what else, cool bush! GF: $25 for all, $20 on Tuesday and Thursday.

The café at the Swanson train station or the Redwood Café at the Swanson shops are good for breakfast or lunch, but after two rounds in the rugged west you may feel like a more suburban experience. In which case you should plan to play the splendid course at the **Titirangi Golf Club**.

This is a golf course some people have travelled thousands of miles to see and play because it's the only course in New Zealand designed by the legendary Dr Alister Mackenzie, the British doctor who left the medical profession to become one of the greatest course architects of all time. Mackenzie designed some of the most famous courses in the world including Augusta National, home of The Masters, Cypress Point in northern California, and Royal Melbourne. He was commissioned in 1926 to re-design Titirangi.

Unlike some country golf courses that play up-and-back on relatively straight, tree-lined fairways, no two holes at Titirangi play the same. On the front nine, recent re-development of the 3rd fairway (new irrigation and new bunkers) and the 4th green (bigger bunkers!) has made this established west Auckland course an even more attractive proposition.

On the back nine the par-5 13th hole, called the 'Wrecker' for good reason, is nothing less than one of the best par-5s in New Zealand. It demands a tee shot from a low tee over a stream and gully of native bush to an elevated and 'blind' fairway. It's a courageous drive too many players shy away from, meaning they wind up hitting the ball too far right where it's possible to wind up Out of Bounds, if not altogether out on a road. And that's only the tee shot.

Your second shot must clear another gully (though one that's possible to play out of) *and* miss a tree dead-smack in the middle of the fairway. But if you make it that far in two you'll have only a wedge or 9-iron onto a green, albeit one with big sweeping bunkers on each side.

The long par-4 17th hole here is one of the most difficult par-4s in the country for the average player. Unless you drive the ball long and follow that up with a monster strike with a fairway wood, you're more likely to go to the moon than score par. GF: $60 AFF, $120 NON. Play with a member: $40.

Redwood Park Golf Club
Web www.nzgolfcourses.co.nz/redwoodpark
Phone 09 833 8253
Email redwoodpark@nzgolfcourses.co.nz

Waitakere Golf Club
Web www.waitakeregolf.co.nz
Phone 09 810 9399
Email waitakere@golf.co.nz

Titirangi Golf Club
Web www.titirangigolf.co.nz
Phone 09 827 5749
Email titirangi@golf.co.nz

Frank Nobilo
See **Local Heroes**, *page 212*

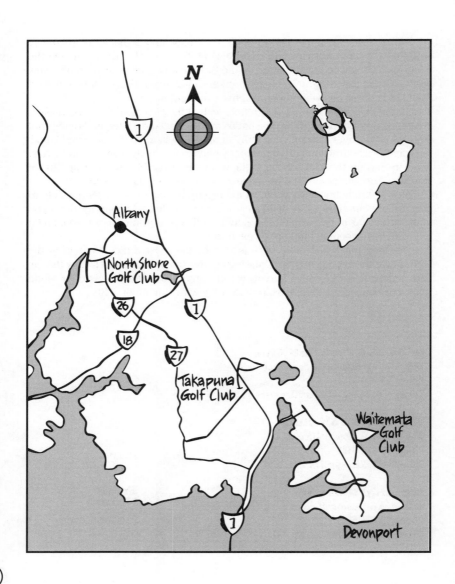

N

Albany

North Shore
Golf Club

26

1

18

27

Takapuna
Golf Club

Waitemata
Golf Club

1

Devonport

Public & Private Shores

The Auckland Harbour Bridge turned the North Shore from a detached retreat into the country's most expansive middle-class suburb. Yet tucked in among the kit-set homes are three golf courses worthy of any mad-keen golfer's attention on a long weekend road trip.

Follow the northern motorway (State Highway 1) north from Auckland over the bridge to the Northcote Road off-ramp. Swing left and you'll see the **Takapuna Golf Club** on your right. For many years this course was managed by the council and as municipal golf courses can be, it was rough-as-guts and in financial disarray. It was under-funded, under-staffed, and under the radar for even the most insouciant hacks.

Then a professional course manager named Richard Ellis took over, raised some capital, and turned it into one of the best public golf courses in the country. Ellis has moved on — he's now at The Lakes in Pauanui — but Takapuna remains great value for money. Management since has continued to make improvements, and it's the perfect place to begin any golf trip to the Shore.

It's forgiving but it's not generous. Hacks will be punished here as anywhere. The front nine is relatively short, but it still demands good shot-making. The par-4 3rd hole, for example, is a dogleg right around a ditch and a grove of gum trees. It takes only a long-iron or a fairway wood to set up a straightforward second shot to a slightly elevated green. It ought to be a routine par-4 for even the high handicapper. But this hole is spooky, for invariably someone from a foursome will pull back on their drive and hit the ball right into that ditch or those trees and end up walking away with a double bogey.

The back nine is long and wide open to the point where it's possible to play a hole from the wrong fairway, which many do. It looks harmless enough until you tee off. Then it turns into a monster. Big hitters will not find Takapuna a threat, just a place to loosen up and pump up the ego for what's to come. The rest of us will walk away wondering how and why this course, seemingly so public, so benign, humiliated us the way it did.

With the exception of the par-3s, there's a kink, if not a full dogleg, in every fairway here. The par-4 9th hole is especially cruel. It's a sharp dogleg right that calls for good ball-striking to reach the turn from the tee and then find a small green with the second shot. Tip: Spend 15 minutes at the driving range here before you play. GF: $23 midweek, $25 weekends for all.

After golf, The Spencer on Byron Hotel is a great place to stay for two reasons: it's possibly the tallest building on the Shore and most rooms come with terrific views of Auckland and the Hauraki Gulf, and it has a cool swimming pool that's perfect after a hot day on the golf course or at the beach.

From there, drive down Lake Road towards Devonport the next morning. Before reaching the roundabout at the foot of Mt Victoria, turn left on Allenby (as in Robert) Road. **Waitemata Golf Club** is at the end on your left.

Waitemata celebrated its inaugural season in 1906, when the site was best known as a race track. The layout of the course today still reflects that history in so far as the front nine tends to play back-and-forth inside the original track while the back nine plays around it.

You'll see what I'm talking about when you pick up a scorecard. This is a flat, tree-lined course that is forever in very good condition. Playing here is like a stroll through a park. If you didn't have to stop a hundred times or less to hit a golf ball it might even be a *relaxing* stroll in the park.

The par-4 2nd hole is the Number 1 stroke hole because it's long (384 metres from the white tee) and because it demands two straight shots (something not even mad-keen golfers can often do) to set up the third approach shot to a small green. The 18th is a testy closing hole with OB on the left, on the right, and at the back of the green.

Then again, its possible to 'top the ball' off the tee at the par-3 10th and still roll it up and onto the green. Trust me. In contrast, Jack Green is a *five-year-old* sensation learning to play here who consistently knocks the ball on the green at the 10th green with a 5-wood. The clubhouse deck is a great place for a snack after your round. GF: $30 AFF, $40 NON.

To find the **North Shore Golf Club**, take State Highway 1 (the northern motorway) north to Upper Harbour Drive. Stay left and try not to be distracted by all the commercial development, for this is Albany, a district that has been so transformed from farmland to factories in recent years that visitors returning for the first time in many years run the risk of mild culture shock.

At the roundabout at the end of Upper Harbour Drive, swing around to the right and head north on Albany Road, the old State Highway 1, to Appleby (as in Stuart) Street about a minute up the road on the left. The North Shore golf course, all 27 holes, is at the end of the street.

North Shore is unique because its 27 holes play in a combination of three different 18-hole courses: the Red, the Blue, and the Gold. All are of a similar length and degree of difficulty. Out the back, this sprawling layout plays along Lucas Creek, an upper tributary of the Waitemata Harbour, though the creek doesn't come into play. But it does give the front nine of the Red Course (the back nine of the Gold course) a unique, scenic outlook.

With 27 holes it's not surprising members have a wide range of opinions on which one is best. The par-4 9th hole is a long dogleg left up a slope that will do whatever it can to spoil a good round and, in an unrelenting way, the long par-5 10th hole that swings around to the right up to a green protected by a couple of greedy bunkers doesn't make life any easier.

The par-5 18th hole is one of the toughest closing holes in the region, because the third shot is often taken from a down slope back up to an extremely elevated green. The par-4 24th hole (when did you last read about a 24th hole?) is a short dogleg right but it's potted with more bunkers than the Western Front. It may be 'target golf' but it's one of the best short par-4s in the country.

North Shore is a private club but green fee players are welcome at certain times. Tip: Phone ahead first and book a tee time, don't just show up expecting to play. GF: $50 AFF, $70 NON.

Takapuna Golf Club
Web www.tgolf.co.nz
Phone 09 443 5502
Email mark@takapunagolf.com

Waitemata Golf Club
Web www.waitemata.nzgolf.net
Phone 09 445 8716
Email waitemata@golf.co.nz

North Shore Golf Club
Phone 09 415 9924
Email northshore@golf.co.nz

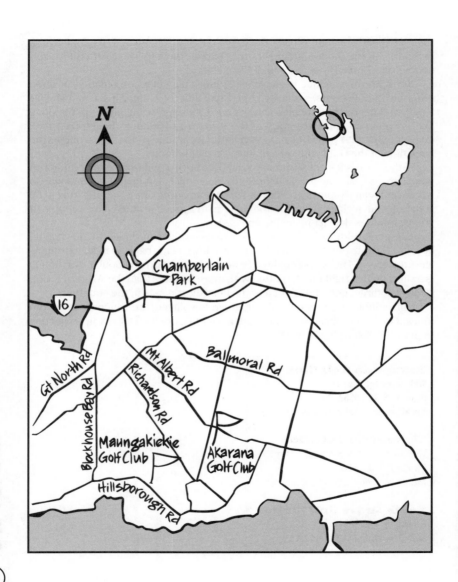

City Lights

Auckland transformed its waterfront for the America's Cup but unlike some big world event sites that turn to dust after the crowd has gone, Viaduct Basin continues to thrive. With the Sky Tower, more hotel space, seemingly endless options for good food and wine, and a new immigrant population to boot, the City of Sails is now more sophisticated than ever.

Make your way on Day One over to **Chamberlain Park**, Auckland city's only public golf course that, like Takapuna across the bridge, has been transformed into a respectable track in recent years. Take the St Lukes exit off State Highway 16 (the northwest motorway), swinging left onto Mt Albert Road to Linwood Avenue and follow your nose.

Chamberlain Park has served Auckland's public golfers well for more than half a century. At a time when most golf clubs were strictly private, Chamberlain Park was a musketeer: all for one and one for all. The motorway extension lopped off some of the original course but the new layout has settled down now and Chamberlain Park is again as popular as ever among sharp-shooters and hacks alike. So much so that the council would do well to expand the parking lot.

Chamberlain Park is known for its kikuyu grass fairways. Kikuyu is a stiff, rugged grass that some would call a weed; but for golfers it serves to prop the ball up, making solid contact with the ball much easier. Yet this is not an especially easy course to play.

The par-4 1st hole may be short and straightforward and some big hitters might even drive the green in one, but it's atypical. Chamberlain Park gets progressively testy through the front nine and onto the back nine. Example: if you are not long and straight at the par-5 12th you have to be lucky with a chip in or a long putt to score par here. The next three holes have a stream cutting across. The stream is more of a threat in the mind than in the hands for if your ball-striking ability is average to good, you should stay dry.

Chamberlain Park is casual and relaxed, if sometimes a bit slow to get around on weekends. But it's the perfect course to loosen up on as preparation for the two more demanding courses that follow. GF: $25 for all, $17 after 4 pm.

On the second day head out on Dominion Road to Mt Roskill. Not far past the intersection with Mt Albert Road you'll see on the left the (slightly hidden) entrance to the **Akarana Golf Club**. Akarana is one of the top clubs in Auckland and the site of a popular Auckland Anniversary three-day tournament. It hosted the 2004 New Zealand Under-19 Championship. It is the club of television news-reader Peter Williams and Radio Sport broadcaster Brendan Telfer. It was the home club of Jim Bissett, for whom the interclub national championships trophy is named, and of Vic Pirihi, a New Zealand senior rep and one of the best Maori golfers in the country.

Akarana has experienced some major changes in recent years, all for the better. A new clubhouse opened in 2003 and the original par-3 1st hole is gone, lost to Auckland's ever-expanding network of roads. Small lakes have been created to bring water into play at the par-3 5th hole and, under the direction of architect Chris Pitman, three new greens, including the 5th hole, were completed in 2003.

Other greens have been rebuilt, leaving the course with a reputation for having some of the slickest greens in Auckland. The new 8th hole is one of the prettiest par-3s in Auckland but the new 12th hole, once one of the front nine, remains the killer it always was. It's a par-5 along a fence line (OB) to an elevated two-tiered green that altogether requires three straight, solid golf shots and two confident putts to score par. Come to think of it, arrive early and use one of the club's new driving bays to warm up. GF: $50 AFF, $75 NON, $30 all day Monday.

Drive back out on Dominion Road on Day Three, only this time drive on past Akarana to the roundabout at the intersection with Richardson Road. Swing around to the right and the first street on your left should be the turn into the **Maungakiekie Golf Club**.

Maungakiekie, the home course of Kiwi professional Marcus Wheelhouse, is the hilliest course in Auckland and second only to Wellington's Mornington Golf Club as the hilliest golf course in the country. Talk about getting up and down . . . the par-4 1st hole at Maungakiekie plays down a steady slope on a fairway that falls off to the right. The par-4 2nd hole plays back up a hill to a green the average player can't see from the fairway . . . and so it goes.

Sometimes, like at the par-4 10th hole where you tee off from an elevated tee and play downhill all the way, that's fine. Its easy walking downhill and letting the old trundler roll out in front of you. Other holes, however, like the par-4 16th hole that plays uphill to a 'blind' green or the par-5 18th that's uphill all the way, leave you feeling as if the course doubles as a site for Outward Bound. Come to think of it, one of the country's finest cross-country and distance runners, Bill Baillee, an Arthur Lydiard protégé, plays here. GF: $45 AFF; ($70 NON midweek); $50 AFF $75 NON weekends.

Of course, it never rains in Auckland, but if it does, drive along the Auckland waterfront on Tamaki Drive to one of the country's top visitor attractions: Kelly Tarlton's Antarctic Encounter & Underwater World. Or visit the much-improved Auckland Museum in the Domain.

Chamberlain Park
Phone 09 815 4999
Email info@chamberlainparkgolf.co.nz

Akarana Golf Club
Web www.akaranagolf.co.nz
Phone 09 620 5461
Email akarana@golf.co.nz

Maungakiekie Golf Club
Web www.maungakiekie.nzgolf.net
Phone 09 621 0093
Email admin@maungakiekiegolf.co.nz

City Lights

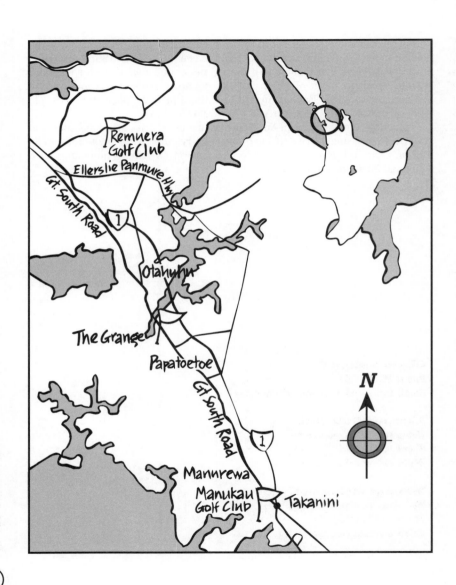

Auckland Traditions

South Auckland gets such a working over for all the wrong reasons it's easy to forget that it's the locale of three of the most established golf clubs in the country. Head south on Great South Road and about a kilometre past the Otahuhu shops you'll see the turn-off on the right to the Grange Golf Club. Check into the Grange Lodge directly across the street then simply walk to the pro shop for your tee time.

The Grange has an impressive new $1.8 million clubhouse, even if one thinks of a 'clubhouse' as a place for Boy Scouts and Girl Guides. But like all three courses on this trip, The Grange is not just about tradition and it's not just about money, it's also about excellence — a quality the club has proven often enough by hosting the New Zealand Open and other international, professional tournaments many times over the years. In 2004 Sir Bob Charles made his final appearance in the Open *50 years* after he won it for the first time. Aussie veteran of many battles here, Rodger Davis, still holds the course record with a 62 he shot in the 1986 Open.

Among the front nine here, the par-4 7th is one that can turn players into raging maniacs. The fairway slopes right to left, effectively 'kicking' the ball in that direction. It's easy enough to drive the ball too far left, in which case you're playing another ball. Drive the ball too far right (as most do) and you can find the ball — only it'll be resting somewhere among a row of trees.

The second shot on this hole is often anything from a mid-iron to a fairway wood across a deep gully to a tiny elevated green with bunkers and shoulder drop-offs on the side. The game-breaker on the back nine is the par-3 15th that, with tall trees framing the approach to another elevated green, makes this tee shot akin to kicking a penalty goal. However, the green slopes so much from back to front that reaching 'the dance floor' does not necessarily mean you're about to boogie-woogie. For any readers who take perverse pleasure in watching a pro suffer, take a position by this hole on the final day of a big-money tournament.

The club recently approved a master plan that will see some major changes to the course, including a new lake, new irrigation and a new hole or two. Stuart Thompson is the ever-popular professional here. GF: $55 AFF, $100 NON.

The next morning follow the signs to the southern motorway (State Highway 1) and head further south to the Takanini offramp. Once off the motorway, the **Manukau Golf Club** will be on your immediate left.

Manukau is where one of the best players in the world today, Vijay Singh, spent a lot of time sharpening his game before he stepped onto the world stage. His uncle, a top senior player, still plays here.

The course sits on the shore of Manukau Harbour. Former European Tour professional, Greg Turner, has successfully re-shaped the par-4 4th hole by the water into one of the best par-4s in the country. It plays along the shoreline or over the water, if you can muster the distance and the nerve.

The back nine here is not as long as the front nine, but it's just as confrontational. The par-3 13th hole is not called 'Crusher' for nothing. And let's be clear: you do not crush it, it crushes you. Just the slightest fade off the tee brings trees into play and should you overcompensate with your swing and pull the ball left, your tee shot can disappear forever into scrub. Moreover, even the best tee shot on this hole still has to have the right distance to land and remain on a small tabletop green.

The club has been around since 1932. The trees are mature and the fairways are tight, but it's an attractive golf course that rightly bills itself as 'a walk in the park', for that is how it feels. GF: $50 AFF, $70 NON.

If you like to gamble or you're just curious to see the greater Auckland region from the highest possible observation deck, then you may want to check into Sky City for a night or if you prefer a little luxury on the waterfront try the Hilton Hotel on Princes Wharf.

On the third day drive out on the southern motorway again, only this time just to the Greenlane Road exit.

Ladies Mile, on the other side of the Ellerslie Racecourse, runs into Abbotts Way, where you'll find the **Remuera Golf Club**.

Remuera, too, has hosted the New Zealand Open. It's one indication of the quality of this golf course, though at the time of my research it was experiencing a major redevelopment including a makeover of all the greens to a standard set by the US Golf Association.

On the front nine the par-3 3rd hole, with Out of Bounds on the left and a bunker looming on the right, can play as tough as old leather. The par-4 9th is a dogleg left to a green so elevated I'm sure there have been days here when older club members have longed for an escalator.

Among the new additions to the landscape, the club has constructed two small lakes on the par-4 15th hole. The lakes enhance the beauty of the hole and, strategically, come into play with any tee shot 200 to 250 metres long. Meanwhile, the par-5 18th hole is one of the best finishing holes in the country. It's only 462 metres long from the white tees but it plays down and around to a green with three big wicked bunkers lurking on the sides. For the average player three shots may still not be enough to reach the putting surface. GF: $50 AFF, $65 NON.

Bookings at all three courses on this trip are essential. Demand is high and, after all, it's traditionally not the way for guests to just turn up and get a game.

The Grange Golf Club
Web www.grangegolfclub.co.nz
Phone 09 278 9777
Email grange@grangegolfclub.co.nz

Manukau Golf Club
Web www.manukaugolf.co.nz
Phone 09 266 8297
Email golfmgc@paradise.net.nz

Remuera Golf Club
Web www.remueragolfclub.com
Phone 09 522 0491
Email office@remueragolfclub.com

Marnie McGuire
See **Local Heroes,** *page 212*

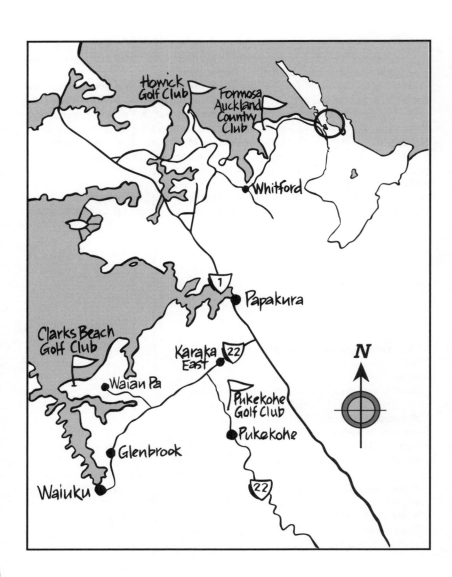

South Auckland Shores

Take State Highway 1 (the southern motorway) to the Papakura turn-off and follow the signs to Karaka, Kingseat, Waiau Pa, and finally Clarks Beach. There you'll come upon a community of homes and baches, shops and cafés on the Manukau Harbour. Maybe it's because it's on the harbour and not the sea that Clarks Beach is almost forgotten and maybe that's the way the people here want it. It's worth the drive to experience this true 'hidden gem' of a golf course.

Follow the road along the beachfront to the Clarks Beach Holiday Park on the harbour. Check into a self-contained unit with a sea view. From there you can either drive or walk to the golf course. The **Clarks Beach Golf Club** is only 5029 metres long from the white tees, so big hitters can leave the driver in the bag. This is a 'short game' course that for those who can't chip or putt can turn into a nightmare. The upside, the dream if you wish, is that Clarks Beach has five sweet par-3s that are among the best par-3 holes in the country.

The par-3 5th hole, to take one from the front nine, is a mere 96 metres long from the white tees. It plays along the fence line (you'll pass it as you move between your harbourside bungalow and the course), but the fence (OB) isn't really an issue here because the green is so close. Or is it? Stand at this tee for an hour one day and I bet more players will *miss* this green than hit it, even though the green is below the tee enough to roll the ball on.

Turning to the back nine, the par-3 12th hole here is possibly the most scenic — but only on a still day with no wind. But when the sea coughs up a breeze some members of this delightful golf course have been known to step up to the tee at this hole with a fairway wood!

The longest hole on the course is the par-5 18th and it's only 442 metres from the white tees. Knowing just the length of a golf course, however, often doesn't tell you much. Water, on the other hand, tells you all you need to know. Clarks Beach has a number of water hazards (other than Manukau Harbour) that can have a visitor smiling and gritting their teeth at the same time.

Once bookings were not necessary, but the popularity of this course, with Aucklanders making the drive from the city, has grown significantly in recent years. The club welcomes green-fee players but asks that guests book a tee time. GF: $25 AFF, $30 NON.

After a night organising your own food and drink (there's a grocery store and café in the Clarks Beach village) depart the next morning and drive back through Waiau Pa. Turn right and follow the sign to Pukekohe where just north of the town on State Highway 22 you'll find the **Pukekohe Golf Club**, a parklands-style course that offers a nice interlude on this coast-to-coast adventure.

Pukekohe is best known in the world of motorsport, for it's here each year where people flock to see the V8 Supercars race. Meanwhile, out on the main road at the golf course, the Canadian firm, Sid Puddicomb, recently made two significant changes to this course.

The lake at the par-4 6th hole was made bigger and a new bunker was built at just the right place in the fairway of the par-4 13th (where's there more water) to mess with your mind — though it's hard to imagine a round of golf at this mature, garden-like course messing up anything. Maybe that's why it's popular with businesses as a site for the annual company golf outing.

This tree-lined course is tight in places, wide in others but it's all kept in excellent condition all year round. The creek at the 13th and 14th holes is Out of Bounds. So is the swimming pool. Say 'g'day' to Craig. GF: $40 AFF, $50 NON.

From Pukekohe follow State Highway 22 back out to the southern motorway. Drive north to the East Tamaki off-ramp. Turn right and head east on Tamaki Drive through Whitford to Beachlands, where you'll find the fabulous **Formosa Auckland Country Club**.

Formosa, designed by Sir Bob Charles, is one of the 'Best of Golf New Zealand' courses (www.bestofgolfnewzealand.com), the site of a New Zealand Open, and a coastal treat. While the front nine plays away from the coast, the back nine plays along it, with a view out to the islands in the Hauraki Gulf.

It's debatable whether Formosa is a links course or not. Regardless, it's a perfectly manicured resort course that (on a calm day) is a joy to play. Which is to say, it's possible here for the wind to turn a casual round of golf into a test of character, especially on the back nine where the par-4 10th, the par-3 11th, and par-5 12th holes play directly into the face of the prevailing breeze.

But then, part of the fun of golf is dealing with the elements and a mad-keen golfer by definition is someone who willingly plays in all kinds of conditions. But let's not go too far with this because Formosa is usually sunny and calm, even if you may not be after playing the par-5 3rd, the Number 1 stroke hole and one of the best par-5s in Auckland. It plays up and around a slope to an elevated green with bunkers on each side. It's a bear in disguise.

Indeed, Formosa is not an easy course to play the first time because it has 'blind' spots and hills and slopes that never stop playing with the mind. Out the back, the par-3 15th hole is one of the best of its kind in the country, for it plays longer than it looks and across a gully to a sloping green perched in the far corner of the course like a platform for viewing the Gulf.

More than a thousand Phoenix palms help make this course unique in New Zealand for its look as well as it locale. Take advantage of one of the resort's stay-and-pay packages as there are 50 very comfortable villas on site, all with sea views. If it rains, visit the on-site indoor sports complex with a heated pool, a spa, and a gym. GF: $65 AFF, $125 NON, $65 overnight guests.

Finally, along the same coastline the more modest and established **Howick Golf Club**, at the end of Bucklands Beach Road at Musick Point, has its own terrific sea views, especially from the 11th and 16th greens. GF: $35 AFF, $50 NON midweek; $40 AFF, $55 NON weekends.

Clarks Beach Golf Club
Phone 09 232 1788
Email clarksbeachgolf@ihug.co.nz

Pukekohe Golf Club
Web www.pukekohe.nzgolf.net
Phone 09 294 8822
Email pukekohe@golf.co.nz

Formosa Auckland Country Club
Web www.formosa.co.nz
Phone 09 536 5895
Email golf@formosa.co.nz

Howick Golf Club
Web www.howickgolf.co.nz
Phone 09 535 1001
Email golfshop@howickgolf.co.nz

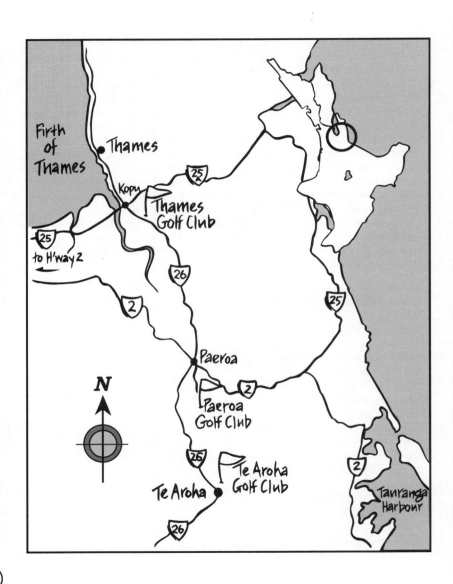

Hauraki Plains

With the Coromandel Range on one side and the Hapuakohe Range on the other, the Hauraki Plains is one big, flat, luscious valley extending south from the Firth of Thames. This trip begins at the foot of the plain, in Thames, where gold mining was second only to Otago and the legacy of the mines remains today in the form of museums and historical sites.

The recent motorway extension and improvements to the roads in the region means the drive from Auckland to Thames takes only about an hour now. That said, readers are urged to be patient on State Highway 2 because that 35-kilometre stretch of road is famous for speeding cars running into each other. From there, however, swing right onto State Highway 25 into Thames. At the T-intersection, turn right and you'll come upon the **Thames Golf Club** just around the bend.

Here, nine holes play on the flat and nine are hilly and a little more demanding, but the bottom line is that long-standing club member Clairice Espiner plays the course regularly, walks it all the way and then goes home to mow the lawn . . . and she's 95!

The course has no water hazards and only a few relatively benign bunkers but the fairways are tight and, of course, there are trees, always there are trees. The 14th hole is a short (102 metres from the white tees) par-3 to a green so elevated that if you come up short your ball will roll all the way back down a slope that leaves you with a 'blind' second shot to reach the green. Once you're up there, however, you may not score par but you'll score a nice view of the Hauraki Plains. Big hitters will enjoy trying to drive over a grove of trees to reach the green in one at the short par-4 12th hole. GF: $25 AFF, $30 NON.

After your round at Thames, check into either the Tuscany-on-Thames or Best Western Shortland Court motels. They are reasonably priced, clean, and only a short walk around the corner to town. For dinner try the Old Thames Restaurant or the Sealey Street Café. The Bakehouse Café is a great place for breakfast the next morning before you check out and roll on down State Highway 26 to Paeroa, only 20 minutes away. If you wish to take the time and you're curious about big, funny-looking birds, call in at the Piako Ostrich Farm near Ngatea. In any case, you'll discover the road is a scenic pleasure in itself.

Turn left at Paeroa onto State Highway 2, then immediately after you pass the classic Criterion Hotel turn right across the bridge over the Ohinemuri Stream. You'll see the sign to the **Paeroa Golf Club** at Rotokohu Road, a little country track tucked in the lower reaches of the Coromandel Range in the Rotokohu Valley.

Paeroa celebrated its centenary in 2004, a note I make because it's not easy imagining what life in these parts would have been like a century ago and what it was that inspired someone to build a golf course here. A hard-luck gold miner, perhaps? A bored dairy farmer? One day I must go back and find out.

Paeroa is a friendly course and by that I'm talking about the course itself, not the club, though the only club member I met was as helpful as he could be. The course has absolutely no bunkers and it's short — only 5700 metres from the white tees. But it's quiet, peaceful, and very pretty. Native trees and bush, flower beds planted by the committee, a small lake, and a stream altogether give this golf course the look and feel of a country garden.

Two long par-4s, the 7th and 14th holes, two that are also the Number 2 and Number 1 stroke holes respectively, are long and tight enough to keep even young guns and old hot shots on their toes. For the rest of us, those of us who struggle with our double-figure handicap, escaping from either of these two holes with a bogey is a fine effort. GF: $20 for all.

Drive on another 20 minutes to Te Aroha, the only town in the country with a quilt museum. You'll know you're getting close to the golf course because you'll see Mt Te Aroha rising up before you. Before you enter the town proper keep an eye out for the turn-off on the left to the **Te Aroha Golf Club**, though, as you've had a round of golf already today, drive on into town to the Te Aroha Motel or the Aroha Mountain Lodge and check in for the night. After walking the golf course at Paeroa, the mineral pools here may be the perfect thing.

Drive out to the Te Aroha golf course the next morning. Tip: Don't drive your car all the way up to the clubhouse or you may be the one to get clubbed. The road to the clubhouse crosses the third fairway. Park where they tell you to park.

Te Aroha is a lovely course of rolling tree-lined fairways and soft greens at the foot of Mt Te Aroha and in view of the Kaimai Ranges. It's only 5200 metres long from the white tees, but like most short country courses, they make up for length by putting trees in the way. Fade or slice too much on the par- 4 2nd hole here and your ball will sleep with the cows.

The par-3 9th hole is a photogenic finish to a straightforward, no-nonsense front nine that plays on the flat. The back nine plays up closer to the mountain and in places affords panoramic views of the Hauraki Plains. The reward for playing the back, however, is the short par-5 18th that's downhill all the way. GF: $20 for all.

Thames Golf Club
Web www.thames.nzgolf.net
Phone 07 868 9062
Email thames@golf.co.nz

Paeroa Golf Club
Phone 07 862 7993
Email paeroagolf@golf.co.nz

Te Aroha Golf Club
Phone 07 884 9656
Email tearoha@golf.co.nz

Hauraki Plains

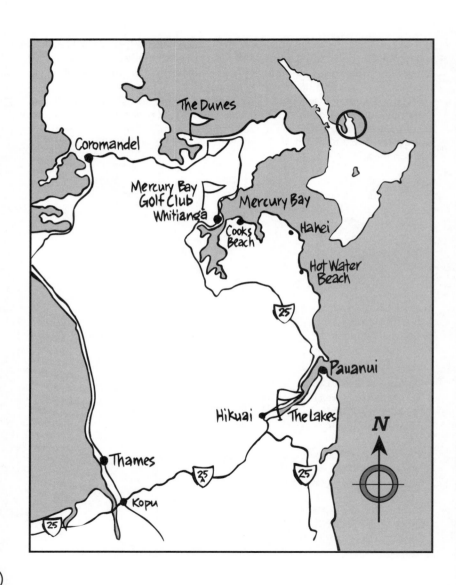

Hippies & Gold

It's easy enough to free-associate the Coromandel Peninsula with hippies and gold because gold was mined here (and to mine or not is still a hot issue) and the infamous Sixties saw the Pacific Coast of this ruggedly beautiful finger of land invaded by varsity dropouts with long hair and guitars singing folk songs and smoking weed. Only now the hippies are gone and the gold is back; back in the form of tourism and intense outdoor activities that include everything from deep-sea fishing and diving to swimming with killer whales. Where's the golf course?

State Highway 25A from Thames over the Coromandel Range is a tight and tedious road but it's only an hour's drive over and around to Whitianga and Mercury Bay. The **Mercury Bay Golf Club** is a quiet retreat tucked into native bush away from the highway. It's close to the hills, but the course is relatively flat and it has only a few scattered bunkers, perhaps because further down the road you'll find as much sand (the beach!) as you want.

A stream cuts through this tight tree-lined course and provides it with character but for average golfers it probably won't come into play except on the long par-4 7th hole, the Number 1 stroke hole, where someone might push their tee shot too far right. A duck hook off the tee at the par-5 16th might also wind up wet. At 5470 metres off the blue tees, Mercury Bay is not especially long. But the trees, both native and pine, that punctuate this bucolic setting have a habit of getting in the way. The guiding principal here, a commandment if you wish, is: hit the ball straight and score well, hit the ball in all different directions and wish you had stayed at the beach. The signature hole is the par-5 5th that's only 375 metres from the blue tees — the shortest par-5 in New Zealand golf, no? It's called the 'elbow' because it's one of the most acute-angled doglegs in the country, too. GF: $25 AFF, $30 NON.

Whitianga is, of course, a popular spot famous for big-game fishing, among other things. Go on-line to www.whitianga.co.nz for the full story.

In any case, after golf drive on through the main roundabout, rather than going into the town centre, to the T-intersection at Buffalo Beach Road. Check into the Admiralty Lodge Motel on your left. The lodge has apartment-sized units and the beach is at your doorstep. The road, by the way, is named in memory of the HMS *Buffalo*, an English trading vessel that sank in a storm in the bay in 1840.

The next day drive up the coast to Matarangi, another holiday playground on the beach, and tee it up at **The Dunes**, a resort course with stay-and-play golf packages that anyone planning a road trip this way should consider. For the purposes of this trip, however, staying overnight in Whitianga reduces the drive back down the coast to the Lakes at Pauanui on the third day. Still, Matarangi, a golf course built as part of a new residential development, has a very fine restaurant and the new three-bedroom villas on the golf course are very cool, self-contained units.

The golf course is like three courses in one: original seaside links, an inland links with man-made water that recalled my visit to the Clearwater Resort near Christchurch (see 'Christchurch North'), and finally a few holes that are more parklands-style. That said, The Dunes can boast one of the best opening holes in New Zealand golf.

The 1st hole here is a par-4, 350 metres long from the white tees, that plays up a wide, rolling fairway lined by tall, trimmed pines directly to the sea, to a sloping green with *six* bunkers. The green is so close to the beach that if you hit your approach shot here too long you'll end up in more sand than you bargained for. The second hole plays among pine in a similar way, but away from the sea. Players then cross the road to where the course takes on its second persona. The 3rd hole is one of the best of the new holes here, even though it's a short par-5. Reaching the green here in two is done at the risk of missing the green to the right and ending up in one of the new lakes on the course, or missing it left into a bunker.

The back nine here includes the parklands-style holes and as part of the original layout it's more settled, older and more ornery, some might say. The par-5 14th plays along the shore and is certainly one of the best par-5s in the North Island. It shares what might be the largest bunker in the entire country with the par-4 15th hole. GF: $50 AFF, $60 NON, $40 guests.

On the third day, drive back south on State Highway 25 to Pauanui. **The Lakes Resort** at Pauanui is on the road into town, just beyond the one-lane bridge. Like The Dunes, The Lakes is a golf course developed to complement a new community. Unlike The Dunes this course is an entirely new 18-hole design, in this instance by the Canadian firm of Sid Puddicomb Associates.

The course opened in 2004 to critical acclaim for the quality of its greens, among other things. The Lakes is the first golf course in New Zealand to use a variety of grass known in the business as L93 Bent, which translates into greens that might be mistaken for a finely made carpet.

But there's a lot more to it than smooth putting. The second hole is a tough dogleg-right par-4 that plays up a slope around a rock outcrop and trees over a gully to an elevated, sloping green. You've been on the golf course less than thirty minutes and you're already two over par. Or is it me?

Rock outcrops, wetlands, boardwalks, native bush, cabbage trees, small lakes, waste bunkers and streams give this course great character, even if it's still only a babe. Cabbage trees are a rare sight on golf courses because they suck up too much water. Here, however, they suit the landscape, uh, to a tee.

The back nine here must rate among the best nine holes in the country, unique because The Lakes is the best example in New Zealand of the newer 'target golf' courses that have popped up in recent years in the US. Hackers and those who do little else but hit the long ball will suffer from the beautifully placed white-sand bunkers and water hazards constantly in play. Bookings are required. GF: $79 AFF, $100 NON. Check into the Pauanui Pines Motor Lodge and, what the hell, take another day off.

Mercury Bay Golf Club
Phone 07 866 5479
Email mercbay@paradise.net.nz

The Dunes
Web www.thedunesmatarangi.co.nz
Phone 07 866 5394
Email thedunes@matarangi.co.nz

Lakes Resort
Web www.lakesresort.co.nz
Phone 0800 184 653
Email enquiries@lakesresort.co.nz

Hippies & Gold

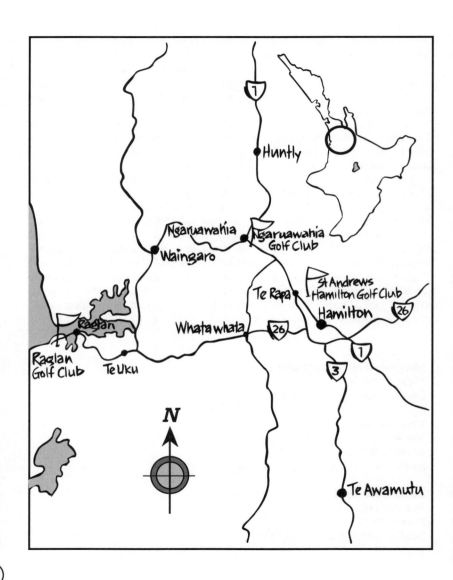

Hamilton North

There's plenty to see in the Waikato, from the World Waka Ama Championship on Lake Karapiro to the National Motor Show to the granddaddy of them all: National Fieldays at Mystery Creek. But if you're looking for something to *do*, try golf. This trip to the Waikato includes one very good country course, a funky little track on the west coast, and one of the finest city courses in the land.

The **Ngaruawahia Golf Club**, home club of Robyn Pellow, one of the top female players in the country, is on State Highway 1 about a kilometre south of Ngaruawahia or, if you wish, about 15 minutes north of Hamilton.

As you drive in you might think: mmm . . . it's flat. But once you're out there having to figure out if the ball should be at the back or the front of your stance as you play up or down a small slope — but a slope nonetheless — you'll see just how deceiving first impressions can be.

The par-4 1st hole is relatively flat, but then the terrain turns into one surprise bump after another. If there's any compensation for a course that lifts and drops like the former riverbed of the Waikato River that it is, it's that the club has created greens so big they could be used for ballroom dancing.

The river next door adds to the country feel of the course but it never comes into play. That is, you won't have to drive over it at any stage. But it influences play on at least two holes on the back nine. The par-3 12th is tough. Pretty to look at, tough to play as it plays along the river, where the sudden open landscape means players can find themselves confronting the prevailing wind. It's one of those par-3s mentioned earlier (see 'The Far North') where some days this 172-metre hole is a mid-iron, and other days not even a driver will get you there.

The par-4 11th is a dogleg right, with a perfectly placed bunker at the elbow before it shoots up to an elevated green. In this way it's typical of every hole here, for it demands both distance off the tee and finesse around the green. In fact, the old river beds have left the course in places playing more like a links.

Say 'g'day' to Kevin. GF: $25 AFF, $30 NON.

After golf on Day One you'll have a host of options on the north side of Hamilton. Stop at the visitor information office in the central city or go on-line to www.holidayguide.co.nz for a comprehensive list of your options for overnight in the city.

Drive the next morning west on State Highway 23 for 40 minutes to Raglan and the **Raglan Golf Club** where even the odd (and sometimes very odd) surfer will give up trying to catch a wave long enough to try hitting a golf ball.

As a New Zealand surfing mecca, Raglan is about seeking the alternative lifestyle near a beach with the only left-hand break in the country. But surfing is not all there is because Raglan has an active golf club that's one of the rare remaining 18-hole courses that still doubles as a sheep paddock. Like some surfers, the sheep are oblivious to flying golf balls. But there they are, grazing next to a tee or green, unaware of the hacks swinging golf clubs who at any second might knock one of them unconscious forever.

Follow the main road into this flourishing seaside town and turn left onto Wainui Road opposite the grand Harbour View Hotel. The Harbour View, with the likes of the Sunset Motel and Wild Coast Cabins, are among the handful of options for overnight should you not choose to drive back the same day.

Drive over the one-lane bridge across the estuary and up the hill. You'll see the turn-off to the golf course on your left. If there is a signature hole at Raglan, it may be the par-3 15th that plays over the estuary. It's the only 'water hole' on what is otherwise a hilly, tree-lined paddock.

The par-4 10th hole tees off from the clubhouse on the steep hill down to a valley of grazing sheep. The fairway swings around to the left, between groves of tall pine, to a sloping green that like all greens here is protected from the vicious sheep by a wire fence. Only one other 18-hole course in this book has sheep on it, and that's at Eketahuna (see 'Wairarapa North').

This is still a modest country track near the sea but tourism to Raglan has inspired the club to upgrade its clubhouse in the near future as part of a development that would include allowing a developer to build new condos. Some regulars are rightfully concerned about what might happen to the sheep.

Raglan now boasts more than a dozen cool places to eat. Vinnie's World of Eats and the Aqua Velvet café are popular. And while you're at it try Raglan's own Gold Beer — all natural, of course. GF: $20 AFF, $25 NON.

Back in Hamilton on Day Three, find your way back to the north side of town and in Te Rapa, off Sandwich Road, you'll find St Andrews, home to the

Hamilton Golf Club. St Andrews was so named because when the original owner, a man named Harry Gillies, built the course it reminded him of the famed links in Scotland, the home of golf. In time the suburb also adopted the name and as if that wasn't enough, many of the nearby streets have golfing names, such as Vardon Road.

In 1911 Gillies sold the course to the council, who then leased it to the Hamilton Golf Club. The course is the best golf course in the Waikato and one of the oldest and best in New Zealand. Turf management here has been elevated to an art form. This is a five-star links that has produced some of New Zealand's best players; namely, touring professionals David Smail and Steve Alker, and New Zealand Amateur Champion Colin Taylor.

The course is bounded by the Waikato River and though the par-5 4th hole is a true risk-reward hole that's considered the signature hole, the front nine altogether might make even the mid-handicapper feel like a pro. But be warned: the course plays increasingly difficult through the back nine.

The long par-4 17th is followed by what might be the best finishing hole in the country, a long par-3 to a plateau green that sits over a brown-sand bunker across the entire front of the green — and the green tends to slope toward the front. At this hole, in 1958, the great Australian Peter Thomson sank a birdie putt on the final day of the New Zealand Open to beat Gary Player and Harold Henning by one shot. GF: $40 AFF, $75 NON.

Ngaruawahia Golf Club
Web www.golfwaikato.co.nz
Phone 07 824 8006
Email nga@wave.co.nz

Raglan Golf Club
Phone 09 825 8483
Email raglan.golf@paradise.net.nz

Hamilton Golf Club
Web www.standrews.co.nz
Phone 07 849 2069
Email golf@standrews.co.nz

**David &
Sheree Smail
Janice Arnold**
See **Local Heroes,**
page 213

Hamilton North

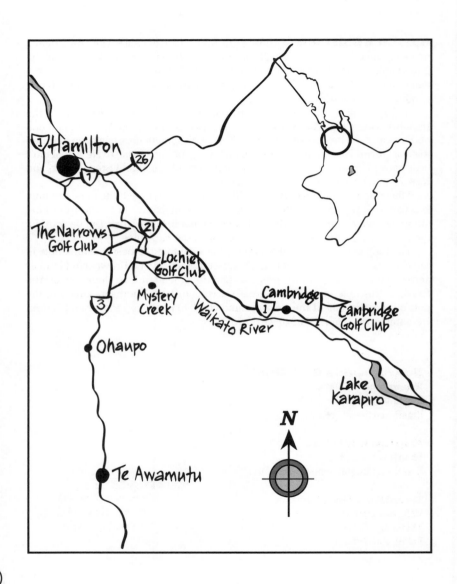

Hamilton South

The Airport Motor Inn in Hamilton (at the airport of course) promotes a golf 'stay-and-play' package for good reason: it's only seconds from the **Lochiel Golf Club** and **The Narrows Golf Club**. Should you stay there you may still have to hire a car because for all the noise the motel makes about its 'golf package', I was told it uses the company van to shuttle golfers to and from the courses *if* it's not being used for anything else.

But because the airport is in the country, with nothing much happening apart from planes coming and going (although Mystery Creek is across the road), you may want to drive into the city after golf. Also, the third stop on this trip is Cambridge so you'll need a car in any case. If you are flying in, all the major rental agencies operate at the airport.

The Lochiel club brochure declares this course to be: 'The Number 1 Club in the Waikato'. I'm sure the members of the Hamilton Golf Club (see 'Hamilton North') would dispute that. In any case, Lochiel truly is a fine course. As if playing the game founded in Scotland was not enough, the club uses (with permission) the coat of arms of Clan Lochiel on its badge.

The course plays over ancient Waikato riverbeds that make it, like others in the region, a course of sharply defined ridges and valleys that can play havoc with your game. But that only means it's anything but boring to play.

The par-4 4th hole, for example, is not the Number 1 stroke hole, but with the river on the left and trees on the right, this slight dogleg left to an elevated green can ruin your day if you're not careful. A grass mound in the middle of the fairway is in perfect position to kick your tee shot left or right. The river is about 10 metres to the left of the green so only the most egregious duck-hook could end up wet. Still, I was told some players manage to accomplish that feat.

The fairways here are not especially tight, although the par-4 16th is slender enough to strike fear into the hearts of all hacks. Trust me. It's long and playing to the left side of the fairway off the tee is a must, in order to set up a clear approach shot to the green. Go too far right off the tee and you'll end up among a grove of pine and redwoods. Redwoods are spectacular trees . . . when you're not looking for your ball among them. It's testament to the quality of the course that Lochiel is a popular venue for national and local tournaments, GF: $30 AFF, $40 NON.

Drive five minutes more in the same direction and you'll find The Narrows, named not for its relatively narrow, tree-lined fairways (this course I would definitely describe as 'tight') but for its location at the narrowest point of the Waikato River.

Its location at an historic ford in the river means that the area was a hub of a lot of activity, peaceful or otherwise, among local Maori tribes. Take too big a divot with a golf club here and you might uncover an artefact from the days when the site was a busy meeting ground.

Ask a member of The Narrows which is the most interesting hole on the course and they're likely to say the par-3 18th because, as the closing hole tends to be, it's just outside the clubhouse. Finish your round and while you sit enjoying a post-match drink you can watch others mess it up, too.

The 18th here plays from an elevated tee to an elevated green — so playing it, and watching others play it, can be as entertaining as a circus. For amateurs it's always unnerving to step up to a tee and suddenly find an audience watching you tee off. It's only 111 metres from the white tees here but the green is like a small tabletop. It's only a pitching wedge or 9-iron away but try finding it when the whole world is watching.

The Narrows is shorter than Lochiel, but arguably more difficult because it is, well, narrow. The par-4 15th hole, for example, is not the Number 1 stroke hole for nothing. It's long, tree-lined and tight, with a small forestry project on the right that's Out of Bounds. Tip: Players who tend to fade or slice their tee shot to the right should have a spare ball handy when they tee off here. GF: $20 AFF, $30 NON.

From The Narrows, carry on north along State Highway 21 for two minutes and you'll end up at State Highway 1. Turn right and drive down to Cambridge, one of the most attractive small towns in the country, and Day Three at the **Cambridge Golf Club**.

Cambridge bills itself as 'the Town of Trees and Champions'. The trees speak for themselves, for here natives and imports blend in well together, while the champions are the Olympic gold-medal winners Mark Todd (equestrian), Sarah Ulmer (cycling), and Caroline and Georgina Evers-Swindell (rowing).

The golf course is located on State Highway 1 south of town. Like the two other courses on this trip, the geography of the course is truly, madly, deeply influenced by the movement of the Waikato River over the years.

The river borders the course and though it's not directly visible, it does come into play in so far as it shapes the Out of Bounds on at least six holes. One of them is the benign-looking par-3 6th hole. The green is about 140 metres from the white tees. The river and OB are on the left and because the prevailing wind tends to blow right to left, it's easy enough to reach the green with a middle iron. You make good contact with the ball and just as you begin to think you've got it beat your ball hangs in the air too long until it drifts left, out of sight and out of bounds in the (invisible) prevailing breeze. Tip: Check to see what the flag on the pin is telling you about the direction of the wind.

On the par-4 11th hole even the most perfect tee shot to the turn of this dogleg left still leaves you with an approach shot to a green that's only a metre from OB.

The course is the site of the annual Cambridge Classic, a tournament for low handicappers that's been a tradition here for more than 30 years. The annual Armistice Day celebration here lasts three days each year in November, so maybe that's a good time to make this golf trip, too. GF: $20 AFF, $30 NON.

Lochiel Golf Club
Web www.lochiel.nzgolf.net
Phone 07 843 6287
Email lochiel@golf.co.nz

The Narrows Golf Club
Web www.nzgolfcourses.co.nz/narrows
Phone 07 856 5207
Email narrowsgolfclub@paradise.net.nz

Cambridge Golf Club
Web www.cambridge.nzgolf.net
Phone 07 827 6381
Email cambridgegolf@paradise.net.nz

Phil Tataurangi
See **Local Heroes**, page 214

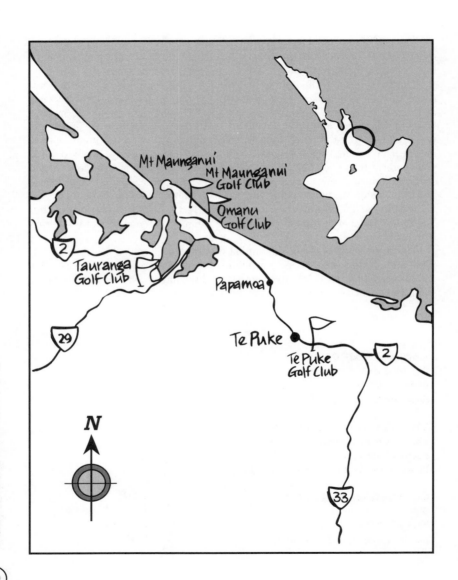

Tauranga & The Mount

The best time to make this trip is any time but over the Christmas–New Year holiday. That's when teenage revellers take over the beaches and the streets and when 'the Mount' feels too wound-up to enjoy. On the other hand, the golf courses on this trip offer some relief from all that.

The **Omanu Golf Club**, a pretty course next to Tauranga airport, is a good place to get loose for this especially long weekend of golf — as this is another of those infrequent trips with four quality courses to choose from.

If there is a single feature that's likely to leave a visitor acting like a teenager on Marine Parade on New Year's Eve, it's a hidden drain that snakes through the golf course. It's not even cited on the scorecard! Tip: Before you play here make sure you ask someone who knows the course where the damn thing lies or else your ball will end up in there more than once, guaranteed.

The Number 1 Stroke hole here is the 3rd, a par-5 dogleg right 500 metres long from the white tees. The drain comes into play here only if you hit the ball too far with your approach shot, for the ditch rests (out of sight) behind the green.

The signature hole, however, is quite possibly the par-4 11th. It's a sharper dogleg right, with the drain coming into play before you approach the green. But generally, Omanu has wide enough fairways not to be classed as 'tight', and for that reason it's a good place to get loose before moving on. If you're still stiff from travel, there's a driving range next door. While you're at it, try lunch or dinner next to the range at the Fresh Fish Market & Cafe. GF: $30 AFF, $45 NON.

The options for places to stay overnight in Tauranga and Mt Maunganui range from low budget to expensive. But for comfortable accommodation close to your next round of golf, try the Gateway Motor Inn on Maunganui Road, roughly midway between Omanu and the **Mt Maunganui Golf Club**.

The course is located on Fairway Avenue, which is off Golf Road and not far from Links Road. In 1935, when the village had a total population of 450, someone thought it a good idea to build a golf links next to the sand dunes. In 2005 the course celebrated its 75th anniversary with much pride, for it is today nothing short of being one of the best golf courses in the country.

All you need to do to appreciate its story is simply poke your head inside the clubhouse. The gallery of photos speaks for itself, many from the 1970s when the course hosted the New Zealand Professional Golfers Association (NZPGA) Championship many times. Look, there's a photo of the great Japanese player Jumbo Ozaki holding up the first trophy he ever won outside Japan. There's one of New Zealand's finest professional golfers, John Lister, winning the 1972 title. Tony Jacklin, Kel Nagle, and Terry Kendall also won the NZPGA Championship here and Bradley Iles is among the most talented young players to emerge from this club in recent years.

Mt Maunganui opened a new clubhouse in 1999 that has grandstand-like views of the par-4 1st hole, and the greens at the par-5 12th and the par-4 18th. The 18th is one of the finest closing holes in the country. It doglegs right to a green with two white-sand bunkers on the right and one on the left. GF: $45 AFF; $70 NON weekends; $35 AFF, $60 NON weekdays.

Escape the bustle (sort of) of Tauranga and the Mount by driving east out on State Highway 2 to the quiet, relaxed **Te Puke Golf Club**, where after your game you can eat as much kiwifruit as you wish. Te Puke is the kiwifruit capital of the world, ever since the 1930s when someone discovered that the mild climate and rich soil here produced 'Chinese gooseberries', as they were originally known, that grew bigger than China.

The golf course is unique insofar as the front and back nine each start and finish with a par-5. That's four par-5s altogether and the longest is only 471 metres from the white tees. Because even the average hack can look good on a short par-5, Te Puke is a relief from the rigours of a course like Mt Maunganui.

At 6151 metres from the blue tees, Te Puke is one of the longest courses in New Zealand. The course had a new irrigation system installed recently so no more will it turn to stone during the long, hot Bay of Plenty summers. The greens here have always been very good and now the fairways will be kept in good shape all year around. A new water fountain between the 1st and 18th holes accentuates the parklands-like feel of the course, one that is further enhanced by ridges and grassy knolls. GF: $25 AFF, $30 NON.

If it rains, check out the cool vintage car museum not far from Te Puke on the road to Whakatane. Back in Tauranga, take Cameron Road north through town past the hospital to Greerton and the racecourse where, adjacent to that, you'll find the **Tauranga Golf Club**.

Tauranga, the home club of 1998 Eisenhower Trophy player Eddie Burgess, opened a new clubhouse in 2001. But it's not the clubhouse that catches the eye here so much as the par-4 3rd hole, one of the most radical par-4s in the country. From the yellow tees it's only 315 metres long for both men and women, but it drops, literally so, into a valley below before it shoots right around a massive pine tree to a sloping green.

The par-3 12th hole is possibly the club's signature hole. Known famously as 'The Knoll', it's only 124 metres long from the blue tees and 103 metres from the yellow tees. But it has a big white-sand bunker directly in front of a tabletop green that slopes from right to left. Miss the green on the short side and you wind up in sand. Miss it on the right or left or go too long and you're left with a difficult chip shot to get up and down.

The tee on the par-4 11th hole looks down on the racecourse and the par-5 13th plays close to the rail, so it's possible to play golf and, on and off, follow the horses at the same time. GF: $35 AFF, $50 NON.

Omanu Golf Club
Web www.omanu.nzgolf.net
Phone 07 575 5957
Email omanu@paradise.net.nz

Mt Maunganui Golf Club
Web www.mountmaunganui.nzgolf.net
Phone 07 575 3889
Email mmgc@mountgolf.co.nz

Te Puke Golf Club
Web www.tepuke.nzgolf.net
Phone 07 533 1832
Email tepuke@golf.co.nz

Tauranga Golf Club
Web www.taurangagolf.co.nz
Phone 07 578 8465
Email manager@taurangagolf.co.nz

Bradley Iles
See **Local Heroes**, *page 214*

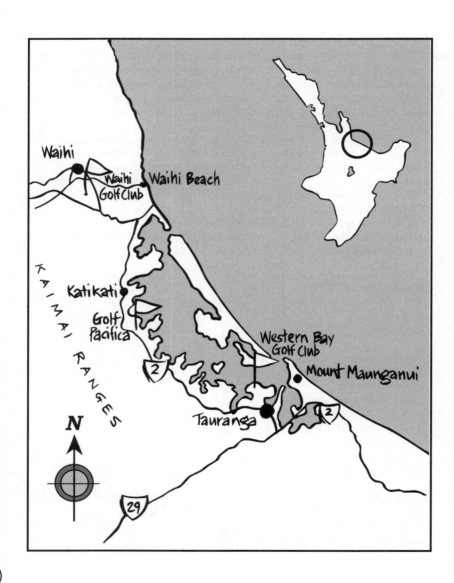

Tauranga West

To play along the compelling Bay of Plenty coast, follow State Highway 2 from Tauranga northwest through Te Puna to the turn-off to Omokoroa Beach. Follow the signs from there to the **Western Bay Golf Club**, a sleepy seaside course that awakened the careers of touring Kiwi professionals Stephen Scahill and Jan Higgins.

Western Bay plays along the Tauranga Harbour so if you stand in the right place you can see Matakana Island and the big blue Bay of Plenty beyond. This is a hearty little links that golfers from outside the Bay seem to hear little about, perhaps because the course is tucked away enough to be detached from the golfing hubs of Tauranga and Mt Maunganui.

People may not have heard of this course, much less played it, but godwits certainly have. The most extraordinary story here is the birds, not the course or a particular hole. Not far away from the 7th and 8th fairways to be exact, godwits arrive from their long journey to breed and where do they choose to settle? On a golf course. Warning: Disrupt the process with an errant hook shot and you're in trouble, mister.

Actually a hooked tee shot at the 8th is more likely to wind up Out of Bounds and harmless on the beach, for this is a true seaside links with all the trimmings. Unlike some links courses, however, where the first hole is often one of the easier ones, as if to ease you into the abyss, the opening hole here can be an immediate and uncompromising pain. It's a long par-4 with a tight left-sloping fairway and a big tree (does it matter what kind of tree?) blocking a right-hand approach to the green. It's one thing for a hole to demand length, another for position, but to demand length *and* position, on the 1st hole? Cruel.

If you survive that with a par don't get headstrong too fast, because the 3rd is another testosterone par-4 — only this hole plays over a drain (Omanu redux). Two decent-sized bunkers protect the green like armed guards. Say 'g'day' to John behind the bar. GF: $25 AFF, $35 NON.

After golf, drive on a little way to the Matahui Lodge in Katikati. The turn-off to the right is on Matahui Road just past the Morton Estate winery. Apart from very comfortable accommodation backed by personal service and fine cuisine, hosts Trevor and Kay Mitchell play golf at your next stop, **Golf Pacifica**. Because Matahui Lodge has a corporate membership at the club, their guests pay no green fees.

Golf Pacifica is a wide-open, user-friendly course providing you know where the stream is. What is it about the Bay of Plenty courses that they like to keep their water hidden? Perhaps it's because the water level was low when I was there but without someone pointing out the hazards, I would not have seen them from the tee.

Still, it's possible to know where the water lies and still get wet. Like at the short par-4 3rd hole, where water on each side leaves only a narrow stretch of fairway to get through. The choice comes down to going for it or laying-up. The hazard flows across at about 200 metres from the white tees. Come up dry on either side of the stream and the green is only a short iron away.

If you do back down from the 3rd hole and lay-up, you get another chance to shoot the gap, as it is, on the very next hole. The difference is the 4th is a long par-5 where laying-up is probably a good idea. Why? Because clearing the water here calls for a drive by someone like, oh, how about Tiger Woods? You play your *second* over the water, your third to the green, two-putt for par and get out.

If you're feeling hungry, the par-5 6th hole here plays through an avocado orchard left off the tee. Should you find yourself there looking for your ball, picking up one or two avocados off the ground is probably okay, picking off the tree is not.

The back nine at Golf Pacifica is longer and flatter and the only water in play is a stream in a small ravine down the right side of the straight par-5 14th fairway. On the day of my visit the sky was clear and the Kaimai Ranges rose up in the distance like a wall that keeps this little corner of the world in sunshine for most of the year. GF: $30 AFF, $40 NON.

Further along the road at Waihi the Golden Cross Mine Walkway and the Black Hill Walkway are just two ways for a visitor to appreciate the town's connection to gold mining. But on a gorgeous summer afternoon it might be better passing time at the beach, for Waihi Beach is as stunning as it is notorious. Or you might play golf.

The **Waihi Golf Club** is on the Old Tauranga Road off State Highway 2, about five minutes south of town. If you are driving in from Tauranga, look for the turn-off to the left just after you pass through Athenree Gorge.

After playing Golf Pacifica you'll be pleased to discover that Waihi has no water and few bunkers. Though it's hilly in parts, it's a friendly parklands course that dips and tucks and weaves in such a way that local knowledge here can make the difference between scoring a dream and scoring a total nightmare.

The fairways are wide and generous enough but the rolling landscape, one that's in transition between the sea and the mountains, has a mind of its own. As it's impossible to know the nuances of this course without playing it for 20 years, Waihi is a stop with heaps of surprises for the visitor. GF: $25 AFF, $35 NON.

For accommodation visit www.waihi.org.nz or email info@waihi.org.nz. Visit the hot springs at Athenree if it rains. The Miner's Café in town makes good coffee.

Western Bay Golf Club
Web www.westernbay.nzgolf.net
Phone 07 548 0384
Email western.bay@golf.co.nz

Golf Pacifica
Web www.resortpacifica.com
Phone 07 549 3412
Email golfpacifica@golf.co.nz

Waihi Golf Club
Web www.waihi.nzgolf.net
Phone 07 863 8678
Email waihi@golf.co.nz

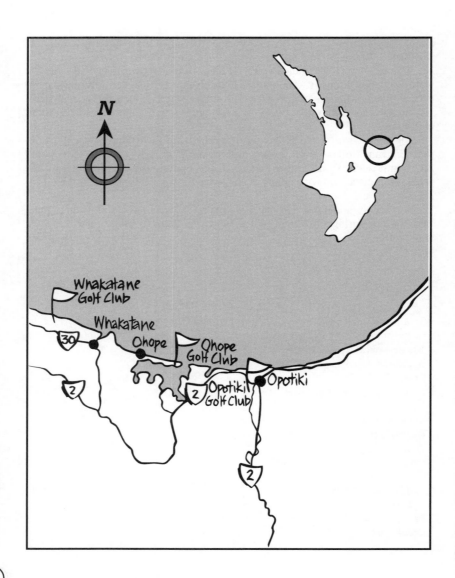

Plenty of Bay

From Whakatane, the drive to Opotiki takes less than an hour on Wainui Road alongside the coastline. You'll see the Opotiki Golf Club laid out over a hill on your left before you reach town. If you cross the bridge over the gentle Waioeka River you've gone too far.

The clubhouse and much of the golf course here feature terrific views of the river and the Bay of Plenty. In this region in the 1860s relations between local Maori and the government were inflamed after a missionary was killed. The government sent in troops to quell a growing rebellion, led in part by Te Kooti. It's not inconceivable that some of the fighting that went on for more than 20 years took place on the site where the golf course is today.

Walking over this course is a treat because it's not especially long or difficult. A new irrigation system has it looking like a botanical garden all year round and the big, generous greens are flat and wide with few tricks.

On the front nine the par-3 6th hole plays from an elevated tee (with views to the sea) down to a big green set in the middle of a natural amphitheatre that's ringed by a garden hedge.

The most nerve-racking hole on the course, however, is on the back nine. The par-5 14th hole is only 422 metres long from the white tees, but it's called 'The Wrecker' because a fence marks a tight Out of Bounds (cow pasture) on the left, the fairway is a dogleg left that's also left-sloping and, assuming you've kept your ball in play, your approach shot is to an elevated green. Go too far right off the tee to compensate for the left-sloping fairway and your ball can end up among pine trees. Big hitters often go for the green in two but the green is small and tight. If they miss the green left . . . you can feel their pain.

Opotiki is only 5300 metres long from the white tees and it's hilly in parts, but the fairways are wide and forgiving and on a good day it's the perfect place to be for a mad-keen golfer visiting this part of the country. GF: $20 for all.

You may not feel like driving toward Whakatane again, in which case check into the Eastland Pacific Motor Lodge. It's one of the best motels around and the owners, Graham and Marlene, are members of the golf club. Try the Two Fish Café for fish and chips or the Masonic Hotel for a full meal.

Drive back to Ohope Beach the next day and check into any of the motels there. Rob Sinkinson, my golfing buddy on this trip, booked us into the Aquarius Motor Lodge, a half block from the beach, and it was fine. After playing at the **Ohope Golf Club** we indulged in fine wine and great seafood at Pier 5. The links course at Ohope is located at the tip of the peninsula, with coastal views in every direction. Some holes are accompanied by the ocean, others by the Ohiwa Harbour, an expansive tidal flat that throughout the summer is a perfect playground for small boats, jet skis, and children too small for the big waves.

When you stand on the 4th tee at Ohope you are standing on one of the highest points on the spit. It's impossible not to stop for a moment and gaze about. Once the gazing is over, however, some players will require a long-iron if not a fairway wood to conquer this long (195 metres from the white tees) par-3. Land short of the green and chances are a definitive left slope in the green will steer your ball into a greenside bunker. But the view is terrific!

The par-5 4th hole is unique in New Zealand because it plays across the road to the car park. Players have to turn a light on and off, as a warning to drivers coming and going, when they are about to tee off.

Also on the front nine the par-4 7th hole challenges players to clear a pond with their approach shot. The pond is directly in front of the green and if there's a slight headwind, for most players it can mean laying-up before the water and playing their third shot into the green.

Out back, the par-5 14th hole has a stunning new seaside rolling green with new pot bunkers. With the harbour and the hills of Waiotahi for a backdrop, this makes it one of the best par-5s in the country. And with the prevailing wind at your back it's not an especially difficult hole to par.

But you pay the price for this luxury hole when you turn back into the wind and play back up the killer par-5 15th. For most players getting out of there with a bogey is a good score. The closing hole at Ohope is a short par-4 but it plays over a deep gully to an elevated green, one of those where too often players see their ball roll back off the green and down into the abyss.

Ohope Beach has a terrific links that every mad-keen golfer should play. If you're playing late, take note of the sign on the gate: Last Person to Leave at Night Please Shut the Gate. GF: $$25 AFF, $30 NON.

The **Whakatane Golf Club**, located next door to the airport, may appear flat and benign after Ohope, because it's a parklands-style course with irrigated fairways shaped by lines of trees that we've come to know so well.

After playing a links course like Ohope, playing Whakatane is a bit like returning to civilisation after being out thrashing among kikuyu and sand dunes. But this golf course is more than 6000 metres long from the blue tees and though the fairways are wide and generous they are loaded with mounds and dips that, like land mines, can blow your score sky high.

The par-4 6th hole, the Number 1 Stroke hole, is a long dogleg right that at 359 metres from the white tees demands the best back-to-back shots players can muster just to have a chance of scoring par. Big hitters and good ball strikers do well here, while the rest of us wind up fighting the usual battles. The 5th hole is a long (184 metres from the white tees) par-3 with bunkers on both sides of the green and only a narrow break in front where the shot that comes up short might roll on. Still, the most picturesque hole on the course, perhaps the signature hole, is the par-3 16th — or do I say that because, at 147 metres from the white tees, it's one of the most manageable holes on the course.

Whakatane is park-like, but it's not a walk-in-the-park. That's why it ought to be played on Day Three rather than on Day One. Warm up for this course elsewhere. GF: $25 AFF, $35 NON. If it rains make your way to the Awakeri Hot Springs 14 kilometres out of town on State Highway 30.

Opotiki Golf Club
Web www.nzgolfcourses.co.nz/opotiki
Phone 07 315 7415
Email opotiki@nzgolfcourses.co.nz

Ohope Golf Club
Web www.ohope.nzgolf.net
Phone 07 312 4486
Email ohope@golf.co.nz

Whakatane Golf Club
Web www.whakatane.nzgolf.net
Phone 07 308 8117
Email whakatane@golf.co.nz

Plenty of Bay

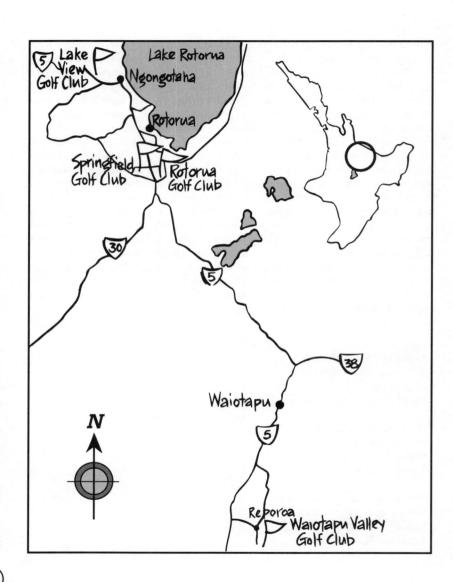

Sulphur City

Rotorua, 'the Queenstown of the North Island' as someone once described it to me, is a terrific holiday destination for a variety of reasons, from its famous mineral pools to Maori culture to trout fishing. But even mad-keen golfers often don't think of Rotorua as a special haven for golf. Judging by the group-tour buses that pull up to courses in this area, overseas visitors are learning fast. May this review change that perception among mad-keen golfers from this country, too.

The Lake Plaza Hotel in town offers a special package for golfers playing three of the courses on this trip, so it only makes sense to research that option first when planning your accommodation. But whatever overnight option you choose (Fenton Street is Rotorua's 'motel row') check in and head straight out of town again north on State Highway 5 and the **Lake View Golf Club**. It's at the top of the rise from the turn at Ngongotaha.

Personally, when I visit a place for the first time I like to get high (pun intended). In New York it's the Empire State Building, in Paris it's the Eiffel Tower. It's a chance to see the lay of the land from above, and with a map it's a great way to establish some sense of direction. In Rotorua, as the name suggests, the Lake View golf course is one of the best spots for an introductory view of the territory.

How popular has New Zealand become as a golf destination in recent years? For some time Kiwis have travelled all the way to Ireland to play, now the Irish are coming here. When you play here, say 'g'day' to Phil, who is originally from the fabulous Royal Portrush Golf Club in Northern Ireland, the home club of popular touring professional Darren Clarke.

I once teed off at Lake View in a morning fog, but as long as the ball went reasonably straight I knew I would find it. The 1st hole is a relatively straight 470-metre par-5. The fairway is banked on both sides by ridges that can even kick a wayward shot back into the middle.

It's debatable which hole at Lake View wins the Oscar for 'Most Scenic' because there are many of them. But my guess is the par-4 6th hole, a long dogleg left, would be a finalist. The par-3 16th hole, one of the highlights of the back nine, is another visual gem that plays from an elevated tee to an elevated green. GF: $25 AFF, $30 NON, $45 if you arrive by tour bus.

Play at the **Springfield Golf Club** on Devon Street West the next day. Ask anyone who has ever played this course what it's like and chances are one word will be heard over and over again: 'tight'. And it's true. Springfield is not a friendly course for players who hook or slice the ball. These intensely tree-lined fairways are so narrow in places it's seemingly impossible for the average player to stay out from under them. A technique to practise before playing Springfield: Slide your hands halfway down the shaft of a 3-iron and practise swiping at the ball like a hockey player.

Springfield does force its members to learn how to hit the ball straight, however, which may be why it has produced so many fine golfers. Foremost among them is Brenda Ormsby, one of New Zealand's best ever, winner of 10 national stroke and match play titles. Penny Newbrook, the 2004 Women's Amateur Champion, plays here and the course boasts a core of super-talented teenagers: you know the ones, the 13-year-olds who make old hacks sick with envy.

The par-4 5th hole here is not the Number 1 Stroke hole but it could be. It's a dogleg right that calls for staying left off the tee in order to set up a clear second shot to a two-tiered green. The par-3 16th hole is 174 metres long from the white tees and in time it may be even longer, mentally speaking, if the club proceeds with plans to turn its low-slung, often-flooded fairway into a small lake. GF: $30 AFF, $60 NON.

The **Rotorua Golf Club** on Fenton Street is commonly called 'Arikikapakapa', or 'the sound of gently plopping mud'. You're more likely to hear mud plopping on the 9-hole 'thermal course' next door (where young Kiwi star Bradley Iles began playing) though Arikikapakapa blows off its share of steam as well. With thermal activity in mind, two of the best holes on the course are par-3s. The 9th hole has a thermal wasteland on the right and at the 14th mud plops up on the left.

Arikikapakapa is unique for all the steam and hot mud. It's a reason to play here. The fairways, ever-changing over geological time, are rarely flat for they are a collection of small mounds and bumps that in places resemble moguls on a ski slope.

Here the ball rarely sits level with your feet. Tip: As you practised the technique for striking the ball low at Springfield, before playing here refresh your memory on how to set up best over a ball that sits above and below your feet.

Arikikapakapa is located across the road from Whakarewarewa, one of the, uh, hottest tourist attractions in the country. GF: $30 AFF, $40 NON.

Finally, if you have time and you're looking to escape for a day the smell of sulphur and the hustle and bustle of tourist activity in Rotorua, drive out on State Highway 5 toward Taupo for about 35 minutes until you come to Settlers Road. Turn left and only three minutes after you pass the Woolshed Tavern in Reporoa you'll see the sign pointing to the **Waiotapu Valley Golf Club**.

This is not a flash golf course but it's quiet, relaxed, and fun. The par-5 10th hole is called 'The Gap' because it tees off between big pine trees and over a death-defying ravine before it breaks sharply to the left. The par-3 12th hole is a plateau green surrounded by a ditch deep enough that if the club decided one day to fill it with water, the course could boast the only 'island green' in the North Island! GF: $15 for all.

Lake View Golf Club
Web www.lakeview.nzgolf.net
Phone 07 357 2341
Email lakeview@golf.co.nz

Springfield Golf Club
Web www.springfieldgolf.co.nz
Phone 07 348 2748
Email springfield@golf.co.nz

Rotorua Golf Club
Web www.rotoruagolfclub.co.nz
Phone 07 348 4051
Email info@rotoruagolfclub.co.nz

Waiotapu Valley Golf Club
Phone 07 333 8562

Brenda Ormsby
See **Local Heroes**, *page 215*

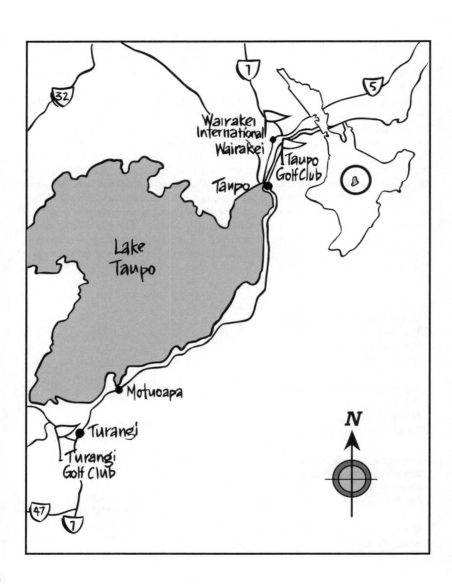

Volcanoes & Lakes

When that famous American writer of Westerns, Zane Grey, talked of New Zealand as a 'trout fisherman's El Dorado', he was talking about the lakes and rivers around Taupo. The Lake Taupo region is still one of the best and most popular places in the world for mad-keen fishers to do their thing. But the reputation of this region as a fishing heaven overlooks the fact that it also has some very good golf courses, one of them among the very best resort courses in the country.

After arriving in Taupo, check into the motel of your choice (and there are plenty to choose from). With luck you'll find a unit with a view of the lake and, at the southern end, the Tongariro National Park. The Suncourt is one with special 'stay-and-play' packages for golfers.

Drive up Spa Road from the roundabout at the north end of town to the **Taupo Golf Club**, one of only two golf courses in New Zealand with two 18-hole layouts. The other is Harewood in Christchurch (see 'Christchurch West').

Tauhara is the older of the two courses at Taupo and so-named because of the nearby Mt Tauhara that comes into view from a number of places on the course. One of the best holes here is the par-4 2nd, for it's one of those rare golf holes in New Zealand where steam vents are considered, according to the rules of the game, an 'immovable obstruction'. I would hope so.

Centennial, the second course, opened in 1997. It's the club's championship course. It's about 500 metres longer than Tauhara and though the par-3 18th (196 metres from the white tee) is one of the longest par-3s in the country, the par-4 14th is arguably more difficult. It's a sharp dogleg left with a bunker in the middle of the fairway at the turn. Nice. Get by that sand trap and your second shot must negotiate a green that slopes from back to front.

This may be one trip where you feel so mad-keen it's worth planning a long week rather than a long weekend. For once you play one of the two courses here, its mighty difficult to say no to the other. GF: AFF $35 Centennial, $30 Tauhara; NON $50 Centennial, $45 Tauhara.

Wairakei International, all of three minutes north on State Highway 1 from the Taupo town centre, was the country's first resort-style golf course. It was built by the government Tourist Hotel Corporation in 1970. It has since changed owners twice and for a while it was almost forgotten. But when its current Kiwi owners took over not so long ago, they invested a lot of time, money, and care in upgrading it and now Wairakei, you might say, is back — back among the best golf courses in New Zealand and the entire Southern Hemisphere.

Taking advice from Michael Wolveridge, one of the original designers, the new-look Wairakei is both more challenging and more beautiful. The trees that blocked the view and divided the 1st fairway are gone, but while the hole is more scenic, in a sense, it's also more difficult with the addition of new bunkers and a rough-as-guts rough all down the left-hand side. At the 1st, big white-sand bunkers flank a two-tiered green that on the best days is as fast as they get.

A new lake at the par-4 8th hole has changed this short, sharp dogleg right from a cute piece of target golf into a monster piece of target golf. Some players will use an iron off the tee but all have to strike a near-perfect second shot with whatever to reach the green in two.

Out back, a new stream on the right-hand side of the 12th fairway has transformed this hole from a short par-4 where big hitters could drive to the elevated green to one where the threat of winding up in water tempers the ego.

The recent changes to this course have not compromised the original layout in places where it matters. The par-5 14th hole is an example. 'The Rogue' is nothing less than the best par-5 in the country. Every mad-keen golfer should play this hole before they die. Here a solid drive sets you up for a second shot around or through (if you're lucky) a tall pine. No amateur *ever* reaches this green in two, so the third shot is up to an extremely elevated, 'blind' green . . . if the shot clears the two vacuum-like bunkers that stare back at you from the front slope. The Rogue is, by the way, the Number 1 Stroke hole on the course, both beautiful and wicked. GF: $75 AFF, $125 NON.

The lakeside drive south on State Highway 1 to the **Turangi Golf Club** takes about 30 minutes. Check into the Parklands Motor Lodge. The golf course is only two minutes away, south along the main road.

If your golf game is off, you may want to try fly fishing in a nearby pool in which case my advice is: hire a guide. But assuming you're still mad-keen after

36 holes at Taupo and having your ego shattered by Wairakei, the golf course at Turangi is a delight.

It's only 5740 metres long from the white tees and it's not especially difficult. From the tee at the par-3 7th hole, called 'The Plateau', players gain a clear view of the lake. The par-4 18th hole is only 286 metres long from the white tees, but it has what might be the only green in New Zealand with a grass mound in the middle. Think of that: you chip from off the green to the middle of the green only to end up in rough. Where's the fishing rod? GF: $20 AFF, $25 NON.

A final note: At the time of my research the soon-to-be-fabulous Jack Nicklaus-designed championship course at Kinloch (www.kinloch-golf.com) was still under construction.

If it rains visit the Tongariro National Trout Centre and have lunch at the Four Fish Café and Sports Bar.

Taupo Golf Club
Web www.taupogolf.co.nz
Phone 07 378 6933
Email info@taupogolf.co.nz

Wairakei International
Web www.wairakeigolfcourse.co.nz
Phone 09 374 8152
Email wigc@globe.net.nz

Turangi Golf Club
Web www.turangi.nzgolf.net
Phone 07 386 8724
Email turangi@golf.co.nz

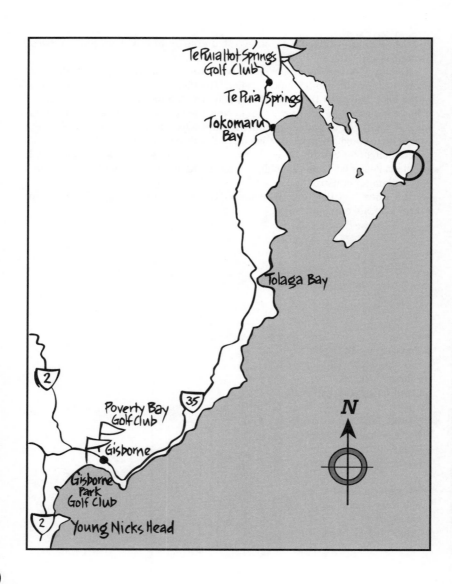

East Coast

Getting to Poverty Bay is a long drive no matter how it's planned, so you may consider flying in and driving a rental car from there. If you approach this trip that way, then as your plane descends into Gisborne, look for the Gisborne Park Golf Club below. It's right next to the airport.

Once you're on the ground and in your car you'll discover the entrance to the course further along Chalmers Road, the airport road. The course shares the same domain with Rugby Park, home of the Poverty Bay First XV. In fact, as I was inspecting the course I met a golf club stalwart named Hank Nyenhuis, a 23-handicap and volunteer gardener, who played lock for Poverty Bay in the fifties.

Gisborne Park is a good course to begin this trip with because it's handy (next to the airport) and it's dead flat. It's a tree-lined course, naturally! Only here the fairways are wide and the trees are planted out in a way that makes them decidedly forgiving — if you can imagine such a thing.

Still, as on any golf course, for it's the nature of the beast, danger lurks. Hook the ball off the tee at the par-4 4th hole and you won't score par but you may score a car. State Highway 35, known locally as Gladstone Road, runs the entire length of the hole on the left and it's OB. On the other side of the same fairway, should your tee shot drift too far right you'll find tree limbs hanging over the right-hand side of the green like a loose lock of hair that (hint) could do with a trim.

The large, dance-floor greens at Gisborne Park are kept in excellent condition all year round and, except for the bunker directly in front of the par-3 14th hole, sand traps are few and far between. To make life even easier still, there's not a single water hazard.

The garden statue of a player you'll see on your way to the first tee is of no one special ('It's just a statue,' I was told). Yet it does add a touch of uniqueness to the course, as I don't recall seeing anything like it anywhere else in the country. It was sculpted by club member Brian Morrissey. GF: $20 for all.

Champers Motor Lodge across the road from the golf course is a club sponsor. That said, many visitors to Gisborne naturally look for accommodation close to the beach. With that in mind, try the Ocean Beach Pacific Hideaway or the Blue Pacific Motel. For a full list of options, however, visitor information can be found on Grey Street. For dinner try the On The Beach Restaurant and Bar.

The next day drive 90 minutes north on State Highway 35 to the **Te Puia Hot Springs Golf Club**. It's a long and winding road but a spectacular coastal drive nonetheless. Stop in either Tolaga Bay or Tokomaru Bay for morning tea.

The golf course at Te Puia is located about five kilometres north of the town centre. As if you might require more than an AA sign, the name of the road is Golf Course Road. Still, you'll make the right turn toward the sea here and quickly get the feeling you're lost. Who would build a golf course here — in the middle of nowhere?

But keep the faith and soon you'll find a true 18-hole hidden gem buttressed by the sacred Mt Hikurangi on the left and gorgeous Waipiro Bay on the right. The clubhouse deck is the place for a full panorama.

The course has no sand traps or water hazards, but the fairways are not generous and the greens are small enough to fit in the boot of your car. But you don't come here expecting a resort course. You play here as much for where it is as for what it is.

Te Puia Hot Springs (if it rains you know where to go) is the only par-66 golf course in New Zealand. It has 18 holes but only 16 greens. It's the original home club of Poverty Bay golf legend Peter Rouse, the president of the Poverty Bay Golf Association. GF: $15 for all.

Back in Gisborne for Day Three, have a tee time booked at the **Poverty Bay Golf Club**, the best course on this trip. The course is a three-minute drive from town. Simply follow State Highway 35 south along the shoreline past the Olympic Pool to Lytton Road. You'll see the golf course on your right. You'll know you're there because Montana Wines has a large plant directly across the road.

Poverty Bay is a links with a rich history that guests are reminded of when they walk into the pro shop to pay their green fees. Photos of the likes of the great English golfer Bobby Locke playing here in 1955 and of Sir Bob Charles, playing here in the 1957 Freyberg Rose Bowl, adorn the shop walls. One photo from 1909 shows women members posing in their standard attire for the day: bonnets, long skirts, and ties. Another, from 1939, shows the course covered in snow!

This is a coastal golf course (Young Nicks Head can be seen in the distance), yet in places it feels and plays like a well-manicured parklands-style course, with beautifully maintained greens and finely cut bunkers. Water comes into play. The par-4 3rd hole sweeps around to the left between two ponds. One of them comes into play again on the par-4 16th hole.

Current US PGA Tour star, Stuart Appleby, set the course record here in the early nineties as an amateur when he shot a 65. GF: $30 for all.

If it rains, explore the Gisborne Mural Trail, the only one of its kind in the country.

Gisborne Park Golf Club
Phone 06 867 9849
Email gpgolfcl@xtra.co.nz

Te Puia Hot Springs Golf Club
Phone 06 864 6887
Email tepuiahotsprings@golf.co.nz

Poverty Bay Golf Club
Web www.gisbornegolf.co.nz
Phone 06 867 4402
Email info@gisbornegolf.co.nz

East Coast

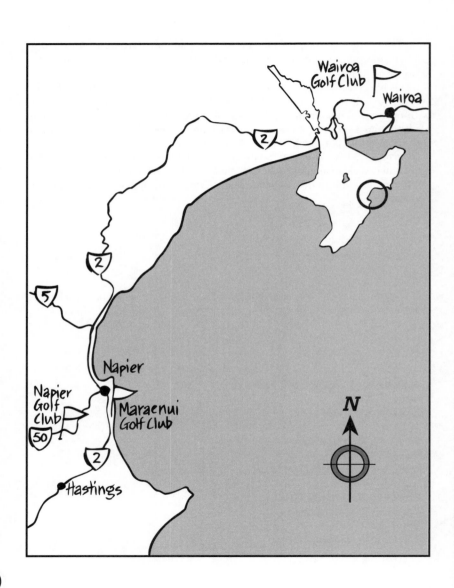

Art Deco

Kennedy Road is 'motel row' in Napier. Take your pick, although keep in mind that Alan and Karen Thurlow, owners of Aces High next to the Napier-Hastings Expressway (State Highway 50), include green fees for a foursome at the **Maraenui Golf Club**.

The Maraenui course is located on Te Awa Avenue, one block back from Marine Parade. As you approach the course, the 18th fairway will be on your right.

Maraenui is only a mid-iron shot from the beach, so you'd think that it would feel and act like a links. But the road between the golf course and the coast might as well be a wall because Maraenui is a quiet parklands-style course that recently spawned yet another young Kiwi tour professional, Doug Holloway, who held the course record of 66 until the Rotorua teenage sensation Danny Lee shot a 65 here in a recent interclub tournament.

If there are two words to sum up this outstanding public golf course they might be 'long' and 'tight'. The course is 6130 metres long from the blue tees but, whichever tees you choose to play from, if you're unable to hit the ball long and straight you'll spend half the time hacking your way under and around trees. The giant phoenix palms here are nice to look at.

The 4th hole, the Number 1 Stroke hole is a long (what else?) par-4 that breaks right and up to a raised green. The green drops off sharply on all sides so if you end up short with your second shot your ball can easily roll back down off the green. Muscle your approach shot too much, however, and it can pitch forward off the back slope and be OB.

If golf photography is your hobby then shoot the par-3 16th hole here. It's a scenic little set-piece with a huge green and stocky phoenix palm for a backdrop.

Maraenui is 'blue-collar'. During my visit some boys, who I guessed were from Napier Boys High down the street, turned up to play in worn t-shirts and sneakers. GF: $30 AFF, $50 NON.

The 90-minute drive north the next day on State Highway 2 to Wairoa must be one of the most spectacular coastal drives in the country. The road curls through the Mohaka River gorge and beneath one of the tallest railway bridges in the country.

The Vista Motor Lodge in Wairoa is the only accommodation in town with a restaurant, though anyone wishing to spend the entire weekend in Napier will find the drive up and back in a day manageable, certainly during daylight saving. The **Wairoa Golf Club** is three kilometres from town on State Highway 38. Cross the Wairoa River and follow the signs to Waikaremoana.

This quirky little country course with six par-3s begins with a short, short par-4. Many players could drive the green here with a fairway wood if it weren't for the massive pine tree standing directly in front of it.

Play a 5-iron out to the left and a 9-iron in and hope you make a long putt because this may be one of the shortest par-4s you'll ever play where scoring a birdie isn't easy. Likewise, the par-3 15th would be a straightforward (boring) hole were it not for a tree directly in the flight path to the green from the men's tee. The women's tee is more to the right and more forgiving.

The course at Wairoa has a drain cutting through four holes, although it's only at the par-5 3rd hole and the par-4 6th where this poses a real threat. The par-4 10th hole requires an approach shot between two tall, healthy-looking cypress trees that form a perfectly natural gateway to a small, tight green. The course has no bunkers but it's hilly; indeed, some members pull their bag behind them on a motorised scooter. GF: $20 for all.

After a long day on the road, a motel back in Napier with a swimming pool is recommended. It's the perfect way to cool down before dinner. Stop in at the town's visitor information office on Marine Parade for a list of restaurants and cafés.

The next morning make your way out of town on State Highway 50 to the best of the three courses on this trip: the **Napier Golf Club**. The entrance is around the corner from the Silky Oak Chocolate Company where the sweet treats are as good as they sound.

It's a small irony that the Napier Golf Club is also known as 'Waiohiki' or 'the water of Hiki', yet the course has no water hazard. It doesn't need one. It plays over some extreme natural ridges that, like fault lines, force players to manage its extremely uneven but compelling landscape.

The course is divided by local roads into three 'districts'. Tip: Use the designated crossings and watch out for traffic. No holes actually play across the roads. The par-4 3rd hole, for example, requires a tee shot to an elevated fairway (if you can imagine) that's flanked by two gorgeous poplar trees. Your approach shot must find a way between the trees to have any chance of reaching the green.

The par-4 1st hole here is only 280 metres from the white tees and a player who can draw the ball has a chance of reaching the green in one. But the green is tucked behind two enormous cottonwood trees that make a direct shot at the green from the tee impossible. The trees are a special point of interest because they're more than a hundred years old and believed to be two of the biggest cottonwoods in the world.

Be careful where you step after completing the par-4 13th hole, for it's there where you'll come upon two unmarked graves. They are believed to be the 120-year-old grave sites of two children of the Tareha family, who occupied the land before it was a golf course. Kurupo Tareha, the paramount chief of the Ngati Kahungunu, not only played golf, he won the first New Zealand Amateur Championship played here in 1903. Today, greenkeeper Ingrid van Steenbergen, one of the few female greenkeepers in New Zealand, keeps the course in tip-top shape all year around. GF: $35 AFF, $50 NON.

Maraenui Golf Club
Phone 06 835 8273
Email maraenui@golf.co.nz

Wairoa Golf Club
Phone 06 838 6000
Email wairoa@golf.co.nz

Napier Golf Club
Web www.napier.nzgolf.net
Phone 06 844 7913
Email napier@golf.co.nz

Kapi Tareha
See **Local Heroes**, *page 215*

Art Deco

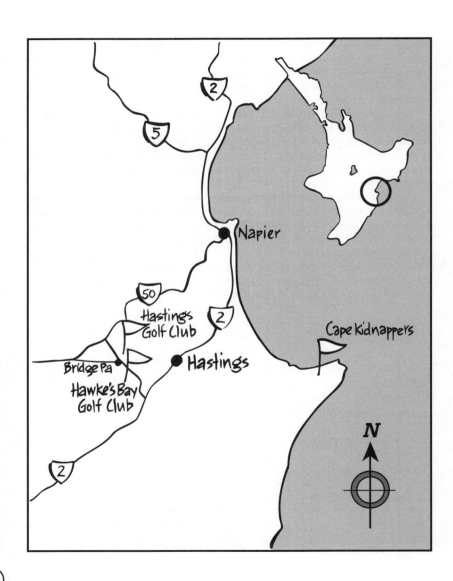

Wine Trail

What makes this trip special is that it's next to impossible to find your way to any of these courses without passing a winery, such is the expansion of the wine industry in Hawke's Bay in recent years. This trip combines the best of New Zealand golf with the best of New Zealand wine and food.

For example, as you drive out Ngatarawa Road from State Highway 50 towards Bridge Pa and the **Hawke's Bay Golf Club**, you'll pass Ngatarawa vineyards and winery on your left and Kevern Walker on your right. The golf course is only a minute's drive past the Bridge Pa aerodrome. Swing right onto Valentine Road and you can't miss it.

This course opened in 1968 and thrived on a membership that depended heavily on freezing workers. The club was a blue-collar response to the more exclusive Hastings Golf Club back down Ngatarawa Road towards town.

In the days when freezing works were fully commissioned the club was flush with members, but that didn't mean the club was flush with money. Because there wasn't enough money to turn it into a full championship course to rival its neighbour down the road, the members settled instead for having championship greens. Ever since, this course has taken pride in having greens among the best in the country. They are large and generous to the point where even the big, sweeping black-sand bunkers next to them are far enough from the putting surface to be relatively benign. With one exception: the par-5 18th hole, a terrific finishing hole with the bunkers cut tight next to a mid-sized green.

The signature hole here might be the par-4 8th hole. It's unique because it has a pine tree growing in the middle of the fairway about a hundred metres from the green. A good drive from the white tees can clear it, only the shot has to be aimed to the left or the right of the tree. Go left and you risk ending up in a bunker, go too far right and you're certain to wind up behind a tree.

The par-4 12th is only the Number 10 Stroke hole, but it can rise up and suddenly take the edge off your game if you don't hit the perfect tee shot. It's a dogleg left around overhanging trees at the elbow and on both sides of the fairway. Go too long or too short off the tee and you're stuffed. This may be the only course in the country with a windmill (at the par-3 14th). GF: $35 AFF, $50 NON.

The information kiosks in Hastings and Havelock North have listings for accommodation. In any case, have your tee time booked the next day at **Cape Kidnappers**, one of the most spectacular golf courses in the world. Built by American billionaire Julian Robertson as a sister to his Northland jewel, Kauri Cliffs, this equally sensational resort course on the outermost reaches of Cape Kidnappers has attracted worldwide attention from the day it opened.

Take State Highway 2 north from Hastings to the turn-off to Te Awanga and the motor camp at Clifton. At the end of that road you'll come upon the entrance to the golf course on your right. It's a private road about eight kilometres to the top.

Designed by Tom Doak, the course is laid out over a ridge-and-valley landscape that, from the back nine especially, produces sweeping views of Hawke's Bay. This course is worth a visit whether you get off on knocking little white balls around or not. Golfers find themselves playing over some of the best fairways and greens ever built. Like the greens at Kauri Cliffs, the greens here are exceptionally quick.

The price of such a panoramic landscape, however, is wind. It might be best to organise this trip around the calmest day possible, for battling this difficult course, even at the best of times, is not for the weak-kneed. But apart from that, the walk is awesome and, visuals aside, the challenge this course presents is the single best reason to play here.

Cape Kidnappers is an extraordinary golf course that will test your game and your sanity. The ravines are deep and the fairways cut along ridges in such a way that to miss the fairway is in many places to lose your ball. The fairways here are not tight and trees are not really the issue. The issue here is losing your focus. With the white cliffs and the expanse of the bay before you, that's easy to do. But do that and this dragon of a course will turn you into a meal.

As at Kauri Cliffs, Cape Kidnappers is one terrific golf hole after another, so there'll always be debate about which one is best. For my part, I liked the long (206 metres from the back tee) par-3 6th hole that plays over a ravine to a two-tiered green with bunkers on both sides and the sea beyond. It's stunning even if I did score a double bogey there. GF: $180 AFF, $300 NON May 1-September 30; $225 AFF, $400 NON October 1–April 30. Cart: $35 per person.

On Day Three, conclude this long weekend with a round at one of the finest of the established New Zealand courses at the **Hastings Golf Club**. If you take Maraekakaho Road into Bridge Pa from State Highway 50, you'll drive by Sileni Estates vineyard on your right and Alpha Domus on the left.

The course, commonly known as 'Bridge Pa', was established in 1898. It has been a regular venue for top professional and amateur tournaments. Sir Bob Charles won four Watties tournaments here in the 1960s. This is also the home club of Stuart Jones, 'The Emperor', New Zealand's best-ever amateur player. At the time of writing he had just turned 80 and had 'shot his age' more times than he cared to count.

Of the front nine, the par-4 5th hole is the Number 1 Stroke hole because it's a long dogleg right, with Out of Bounds on the right of the entire fairway. Only the best players reach this green in two and even they have to deal with a two-tiered green that's not easy to read. The club shows its sense of mercy on this hole, however, by not having bunkers.

Out the back, at the short par-4 12th (310 metres from the white tees), a fairway wood or a long-iron off the tee is all that's required to be in a good position for your approach. But the second shot is up a slope to a raised green that drops off steeply on all sides. The par-4 18th here is a picturesque finishing hole directly in front of the clubhouse where, if 'The Emperor' is watching, you should feel nervous. Real nervous. GF: $50 AFF, $80 NON.

Hawke's Bay Golf Club
Web www.hawkesbaygolfclub.co.nz
Phone 06 879 8890
Email hawkes.bay@golf.co.nz

Cape Kidnappers
Web www.capekidnappers.com
Phone 06 875 1900
Email proshop@kidnappers.com

Hastings Golf Club
Web www.hastingsgolfclub.co.nz
Phone 06 879 7382
Email gm.hgc@xtra.co.nz

Stuart Jones
See **Local Heroes**, *page 216*

Wine Trail

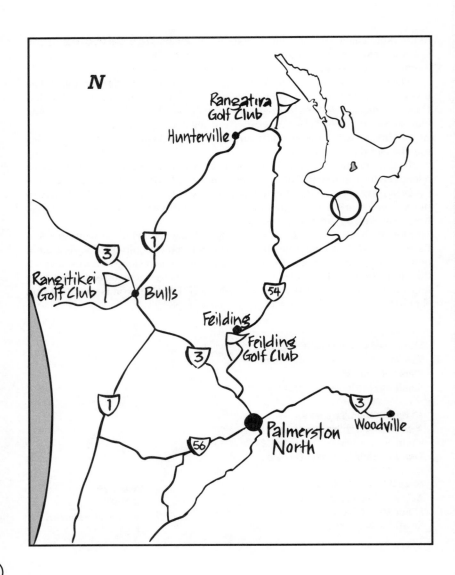

Manawatu West

Take State Highway 54 from Palmerston North to Feilding and the **Feilding Golf Club** will be on your left before you reach this charming town, known for its wide streets and Edwardian buildings. Ask someone why Feilding is spelled 'wrong' and the response might be: because that's the way it's always been. So now, let the record show that the town is named after Colonel William Feilding, a director of the Emigrants and Colonists Aid Corporation who managed the new European settlement here in 1874 — and that's the way he spelled his name!

Meanwhile, the golf course is a stock parklands-style course defined by trees to such an extent that some players may finish their round and wish they had brought along a chainsaw too. The course is not especially long — 5731 metres for men, 5555 metres for women — but the key to scoring well here is not going long so much as being straight. The average golfer might do best by keeping the driver in the bag.

The par-5 3rd hole, for example, is only 426 metres long, a slight dogleg right to a long, narrow green. There's no sand to get in the way of big hitters who often cut the corner (go over trees) to reach the green in two. For them it's a driver and a 7-iron into the green. For the rest of us, try a fairway wood off the tee just to keep the ball in play, for that's all that's required here and elsewhere on this course to score well.

On the back nine the 14th hole is another short par-5 (427 metres from the white tees) and John Daly wannabes can reach the green in two, at the risk of sending their approach shot too far right over a stopbank and OB. Keep the ball in the fairway with the first two shots and the third shot takes that risk out of the mix. Easy.

The course plays alongside a tributary of the Rangitikei River and is kept in very good nick all year round. GF: $25 AFF, $35 NON.

Drive back into Palmerston North for the night. The Albert Motor Lodge on Main Street has a dedicated sports bar, though if you wish to be more centrally located, check out 'motel row' on Fitzherbert Avenue. Here the options range from the modest three-star motel to the five-star with all the bells and whistles. For dinner try the Mexican restaurant on the corner of Fitzherbert and Ferguson.

Drive north the next morning on State Highway 1, where just north of Hunterville you come across one of the most interesting golf courses in New Zealand at the **Rangatira Golf Club**. Rangitira is a must-play and remember to bring your camera. The panoramic views of the Rangitikei River and its extraordinary white cliffs give this modest golf track a backdrop like no other.

The course is laid out over three levels, and terraced in a way that has been defined by the movement of the river over many years. Consequently, there's no other golf course like it in the country. The first six holes play along the top, the next six holes play across a 'second floor', and the last six holes play around a bottom floor, face-to-face with the river if you will. (Though the river doesn't come into play.)

Here, when players complete their round they ride an ingenious cable-car back to the top. The cab holds up to four adults with their clubs and there's no extra charge! The property as a whole is a study in native trees. And please, leave the wood pigeons in peace. It's their home, after all. GF: $20 for all.

Drive back to Palmerston North for the night. If you're feeling peckish pick up a kebab from Jabies in Bulls. Palmerston North is now the home of the New Zealand rugby museum and museums devoted to horse-drawn vehicles and steam trains. You may want to make a museum stop whether it rains or not.

In any event, drive back out to Bulls on the third day; only this time, rather than turning right and heading north on State Highway 1, turn left and follow that road around to the **Rangitikei Golf Club**, a course US PGA Tour player Craig Perks, originally from the Manawatu, has called 'my favourite golf course anywhere in the world'. At least that's what he wrote on a photo of himself winning the 2002 Players Championship that's taped to a window of the clubhouse.

Rangitikei is a true links with sand mounds, kikuyu, windswept pohutukawa . . . the works. The tee boxes here are commonly elevated but that's not really any kind of advantage because the fairways roll and drop and rise up again over mounds in such an irregular way that local knowledge means everything. For example, it helps to know where you're going at the par-4 6th hole, as it's a 'blind' tee shot over a hill. On second thought, you have to climb the wooden ladder to see that the fairway is clear before you tee off anyway.

The fairway of the par-4 18th hole has so many small mounds popping up all over it that it looks like it's suffering from disease — a monster from a B-grade horror movie. It's 338 metres long from the white tees and not a piece of flat earth in sight.

Rangitikei is a true links that's great fun. I can see why Craig Perks thinks of it the way he does. GF: $20 for all.

Feilding Golf Club
Web www.feilding.nzgolf.net
Phone 06 323 5976
Email feilding@golf.co.nz

Rangatira Golf Club
Web www.rangatiragolf.co.nz
Phone 06 322 9859
Email secretary@rangatiragolf.co.nz

Rangitikei Golf Club
Web www.rangitikeigolf.co.nz
Phone 06 322 1475
Email rangitikeigolf@paradise.net.nz

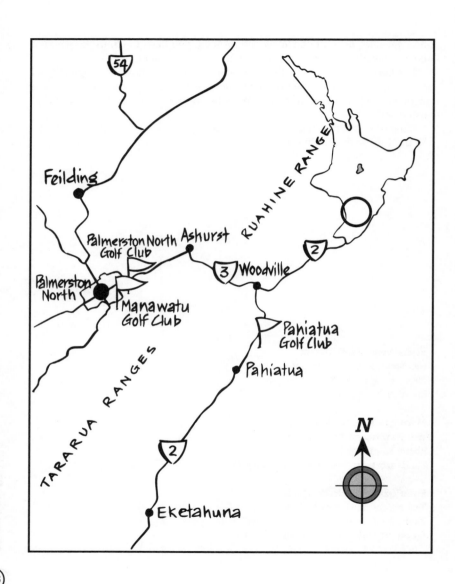

Manawatu East

Is there anyone left in the Western world under the age of 60 who plans a holiday without first doing some internet research? I don't think so. Even a simple three-day golf trip to the lower North Island these days means going on-line first.

Go to www.manawatu.com and you'll find information on everything there is in and around Palmerston North, from New Zealand's only professional theatre outside the four major cities to Cosmetic Dental Care. Click on 'Golf', however and, in my case anyway, up popped the name of a motel. Strange.

But I knew I'd find something on Fitzherbert Avenue, Palmy's 'motel row'. What I was more interested in was finding my way to the **Palmerston North Golf Club**. Turns out it's north on Main Street past Memorial Park. Turn right at Bridgewater Terrace and the golf course is at the end of the street.

The Palmerston North course is by the Manawatu River, but not of it. By that I mean the river itself does not come into play. Okay, so the par-5 3rd hole here is a dogleg left that plays next to the river. But even a high handicapper would have to *want* to hit a ball in the river to reach it.

The river has produced a lagoon, however, that encircles the entire course and comes into play on the back nine. The par-5 14th hole is not called 'Waterloo' for nothing. Come up short on either your second or third shot and you'll wind up in the drink. The lagoon flows in front of the green.

Your tee shot at the short par-4 15th hole must clear the lagoon, though for the average player this should not be a problem because the lagoon is close to the tee. Still, it's a dogleg left where big hitters like to carry the water and cut the corner to try to reach the putting surface in a single blow.

Palmerston North is a casual, tree-lined parklands course just right for getting loose after being in the car. Tip: Keep your eyes peeled when you drive in. The par-3 6th hole and the par-3 17th (with four bunkers) play across the road. GF: $25 AFF, $30 NON.

On Day Two follow State Highway 3 north to Woodville. Turn south from there onto State Highway 2 to the **Pahiatua Golf Club**. It's about a 30-minute drive altogether and the road through the Manawatu River gorge is jaw-dropping if you're seeing the gigantic windmills of the Te Apiti Wind Farm for the first time.

Pahiatua is flat with big, circular greens carved out of verdant fairways. Players who still haven't learned the techniques for hitting a ball lying in sand should do well here because the course has only two bunkers.

Grassy swells, an altogether irregular landscape, and a couple of interesting doglegs make up for that. The par-4 3rd hole, for instance, is a sharp dogleg left around a ridge and tall gum trees. When a northerly blows, big hitters direct their tee shot over the ridge and to the left of the trees hoping the wind will blow their ball back right and down onto the green in one! It's a hell of a shot when it works and a signature hole if there ever was one.

The stream at the back of the course doesn't really come into play, but it's close to the par-3 9th hole. Here, from an elevated tee to a green with a bunker in front, club member Neville Baldwin scored his only hole-in-one! GF: $15 AFF, $20 NON.

You'll get a second and more panoramic look at the wind farm and the Manawatu Gorge on your drive from Pahiatua back to Palmerston North, where on Day Three you have a tee time booked at the **Manawatu Golf Club**.

Manawatu is the home course of some of the best players New Zealand has ever produced; namely, Grant Waite, Craig Perks, and Tim Wilkinson. Manawatu and Otago have an ongoing feud as to which golf club is the oldest and while it's generally accepted that Otago is the oldest club in the country, Manawatu is (and I quote from club literature) 'the oldest course still on its original site'. Fine. Suffice it to say, like 'Balmacewen', as the Otago Golf Club is commonly called, 'Hokowhitu', as the course at Manawatu is known, is one of the best courses in the country, regardless of age.

The Manawatu Golf Club is located on Centennial Drive (off Albert Street) close to the river and in the heart of a quiet suburb. The course is beautifully kept and its signature trees — tall eucalyptus and Phoenix palms — immediately catch the eye. Tim Wilkinson, about to begin a new year on the US PGA Nationwide Tour, happened to be in the pro shop the day I stopped by. He has many favourite holes on the course but he highlighted for me the par-4 10th hole that plays down a slope and then back up a hill to a green that slopes off severely at the back. All this and more when it's played into the face of one of those stiff Manawatu winds.

The course, with a view of the Ruahine Range in the distance, has hosted five New Zealand Opens and seven New Zealand Amateur championships. Sir Bob Charles won the last of his four Opens here. GF: $30 AFF, $50 NON.

If it rains, Palmerston North has its share of sports bars or you could visit the New Zealand Rugby Museum on Cuba Street (www.rugbymuseum.co.nz). The Tokomaru Steam Engine Museum has the country's largest collection of working steam trains (www.tokomarusteam.com). Then again, you could revisit the website mentioned earlier and have work done on your teeth.

Palmerston North Golf Club
Web www.pngolf.co.nz
Phone 06 351 0700
Email palmerston.north@golf.co.nz

Pahiatua Golf Club
Phone 06 376 8005
Email pahiatua@golf.co.nz

Manawatu Golf Club
Web www.manawatu.nzgolf.net
Phone 06 357 8793
Email gm@manawatugolfclub.com

Craig Perks
Grant Waite
See **Local Heroes**,
page 217

Manawatu East

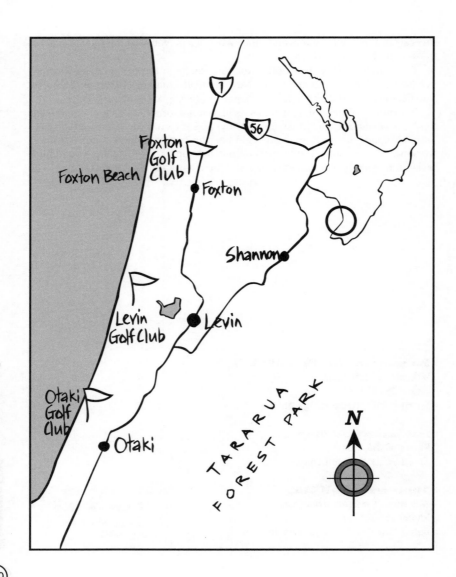

Horowhenua

The estuary of the Manawatu River at Foxton is one of the most highly prized wetlands in the country and accordingly it's become a bird sanctuary with plenty of national and international interest. During the summer months it's home to a number of rare and endangered birds, the most famous being the godwit, which flies 14,000 kilometres non-stop from the Arctic Circle to reach Foxton, of all places.

Golfers do not have to go to such extremes to play there. The **Foxton Golf Club** is located on State Highway 1 just north of town. You'll know you're close when you see de Molen, an enormous Dutch-style windmill — the biggest windmill in the country I'm sure.

Foxton is only five kilometres from the sea, so it's should come as no surprise that the course feels like a links and in places it definitely looks like a links. But more often than not it plays like a course in the country (for example, on normal grass) because the club recently installed a new irrigation system that keeps the fairways looking green in summer.

The par-4 2nd hole here is the Number 1 Stroke hole, not because it's especially long but because it's a split-level fairway and dogleg left that requires virtually a dead-straight tee shot on the right line to put your ball in the best position for an approach to the green. Go straight but too short and your approach will be blocked by trees. Go straight but too long and you'll have to negotiate your way back through trees shaping the fairway on the right.

But it's the par-3 10th hole that some club members say is their favourite hole. It's only 124 metres from the men's and the women's tees, but someone once decided to make it more complicated by planting a tree in the line of fire.

Further, the green has a small bunker front right and a grassy knoll on the left. If background movement bothers you this hole will be your worst nightmare thanks to the flow of traffic on State Highway 1 at the back.

The par-5 18th hole here is a good closing hole. It's not long, but it's made tight by overhanging pine trees flanking the green. Then again, maybe by the time you play here someone will have trimmed them back. A small memorial on this hole marks the spot where a popular Manawatu golfer, Lou Hubbard, died with his boots on. GF: $15 AFF, $20 NON.

The **Levin Golf Club** further down the main road is found off the main highway between Lake Horowhenua (famous locally for eels) and Hokio Beach, about five kilometres west of town. Accordingly, it might be the quietest golf course on the planet. Play Levin and by the time you reach the back nine the sound of your club striking the ball will seem loud.

Levin is a links with sandy soil that drains so well it's possible to play here even after those heavy Horowhenua rains that have caused some serious flooding in these parts in the past. In its early days, the club had a scheme that kept the course looking tidy and raised money for the club at the same time: sheep. The sheep kept the grass down until they were sold off. I forgot to ask, but my guess is the club got back lamb chops to raffle off for still more income.

The sheep are gone now and though the club has had to find new ways of generating income, the course has never looked better. Many of the holes are framed by small dunes that, like high embankments, define the shape of fairways.

The par-5 4th hole sweeps right, to a green with one lone cabbage tree in front of it. My personal favourite hole was the par-4 17th. It's not long (big hitters can drive it) but it plays up a slope to a narrow green that's skewed left so that only a perfect drive could avoid the two bunkers in front or the steep shoulder drop-off on the left and out the back. The back tee at the par-4 15th hole is the place to stop for the only view of Levin and the Tararua Range. GF: $25 for all.

For an overnighter by the sea, try the Waitarere Beach motor camp. The Hot Plate in Levin serves traditional Kiwi fare. Try Rangoli's if you're feeling 'ethnic'. Stop at the Station House in the morning for coffee before heading down the road to Otaki.

Otaki, as any pedantic schoolmaster will tell you, is Kapiti Coast and not Horowhenua. But for a long weekend golf trip, the **Otaki Golf Club** is a logical end point (or starting point) for a weekend that includes the two courses above. The drive between Otaki and Levin, after all, is about as long as it will take you to play the par-5 1st hole at Otaki — unless there's a prevailing wind, in which case, it's quicker driving to Levin.

To what extent a golf course is a links or something else is debatable, but for me the sure sign of a links is kikuyu. Indeed, playing on kikuyu is compensation for the sand and wind and rough that true links courses put in front of you. This strain of grass is so tough it acts like a tee by keeping the ball off the ground, making good contact easier. That is Otaki and more.

Otaki is shaped by sand dunes, young and old, that make it especially fun to play. The greens tend to be small or narrow with little room for error and the landscape changes its appearance magically depending on the angle of the sun. This is a west coast links (Muriwai Beach is another) that's especially beautiful in the orange and golden light of a late-afternoon summer sun.

As a tribute to the famous azalea beds at Augusta National, home of The Masters, Otaki has planted azaleas too. Or is that to compensate for the unsightly power lines that cut across the course at the 1st and 18th holes?

Otaki is a modest links close to the town's dramatic beach. But please, as the sign says, no playing in jandals, singlets, or beach shorts. GF: $20 midweek, $25 weekends, for all.

Foxton Golf Club
Web www.foxtongolf.co.nz
Phone 06 363 8160
Email foxtongolfclub@paradise.net.nz

Levin Golf Club
Web www.levinlinksgolf.co.nz
Phone 06 368 6189
Email golf@levinlinksgolf.co.nz

Otaki Golf Club
Web www.otakigolfclub.co.nz
Phone 06 364 8260
Email info@otakigolfclub.co.nz

Horowhenua

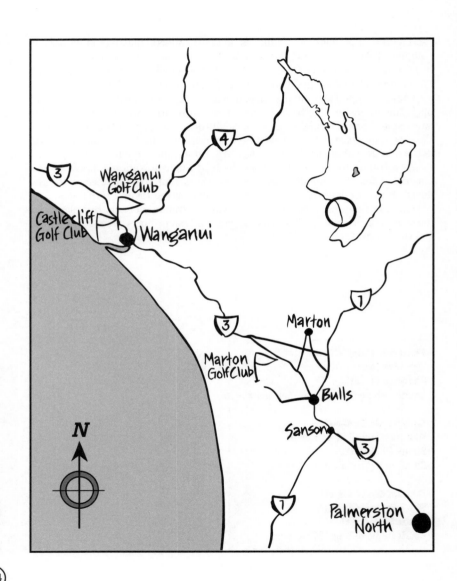

River City

Drive east from Palmerston North on State Highway 3 towards Wanganui and about five minutes after passing through Bulls you'll see the turn left to the **Marton Golf Club**, your 'warm-up' round for the next two days playing in Wanganui. This is not to suggest the course at Marton is easier than the two in the River City, for as one member here I spoke to said, 'If you can score well here, you can score even better there [Wanganui], because this is the hardest of the three courses.'

I leave degree of difficulty for you to decide. Marton is a wonderful 6000 metre (from the back tees) links with all the trappings — dunes, elevated tees, and extremely rolling fairways with mounds that will inevitably deflect your ball where you don't want it to go. But length alone is never a measure of difficulty.

The par-3 6th hole at Marton is not as easy to conquer as its Number 17 Stroke rating suggests. It's only 131 metres long from the white tees and 103 metres long from the yellow tees, but it has multiple bunkers staring back and a steep bank at the back of the green. If you're too short you end up in sand, if you're too long you're forced to chip back up a ski slope. It's a true devil in disguise.

The par-4 15th hole is less than 300 metres long, but it's a slight dogleg left over a clump of trees. Big hitters invariably try to clear the trees to reach the green in one, the rest of us play it safe with a driver or fairway wood to the elbow and, say, a 7-iron in from there.

Marton reminded me why I don't like pine trees on golf courses: because the greens below are invariably covered with annoying needles that have to be brushed off the line of every putt. At moments like that I have to tell myself: relax dude, you're on holiday. GF: $20 for all.

From Marton it's a short drive to Wanganui. If you haven't booked a place to stay, cross the river at the Cobham Bridge, turn right onto Heads Road and that will take you to Guyton Street where you'll find a useful visitor information centre with a listing of accommodation. As this is the River City, try the Riverside Motel as I did — because it had a bottle store next door.

The next morning follow Heads Road along the river to the **Castlecliff Golf Club**, another terrific links like Marton. Castlecliff is a bit shorter than Marton and since many of the pine trees have been taken out over the years it's become more forgiving. Even the ugliest mis-hit will still be in play. Trust me.

Castlecliff is where the Owen brothers, Simon, Craig, and Paul, began playing golf. Simon became one of New Zealand's finest touring professionals, finishing a hard-luck second to Jack Nicklaus one year at the British Open. Craig is still one of the country's top senior tour players who, not long before I met him at the Westown Golf Club in New Plymouth where he's now based, won a tournament in Tasmania. Paul now looks after the Te Ngutu Golf Club (see 'Taranaki Country'). Meanwhile, back at Castlecliff, Simon and Craig share the course record of 66.

Castlecliff is situated on the Tasman Sea. A series of holes with elevated tees afford great views even if they won't do much for your game. Local knowledge is important, so before you play ask someone who knows the course what the tricks are.

Stand on the elevated tee at the par-3 9th (a 9th that's as far away from the clubhouse as you can get) and you might think you're playing in Scotland. Indeed, how you approach any of the holes on this course, but especially the par-3s, will depend on the conditions. If the wind is up the par-3 15th, for example, it turns from Jekyll into Hyde (no relation). GF: $20 AFF, $25 NON.

Spend the evening in town strolling along Victoria Avenue and checking out the trail of Wanganui's heritage buildings. Pick up some takeaways along the way. The next morning drive west on State Highway 3 up St Johns Hill to Montgomery Road. There you'll swing left to the **Wanganui Golf Club**, commonly known as 'Belmont Links'.

As their amateur and then professional careers developed, the Owen brothers played most of their golf here, probably because Belmont is simply one of the best golf courses in the country. The modern clubhouse rests on a hill overlooking the course below.

Though Belmont is called a links it's got quite a different character to Castlecliff. Indeed, the club recently installed a new irrigation system and the course is so well maintained generally that in places it plays more like a course in the country.

The par-4 6th hole provides a view of Wanganui while the par-3 5th is called

'Sea View' for obvious reasons. Yet this is not a course you play for the views. You play it for what it is: a top course with a rich history. Belmont has hosted six New Zealand Open Championships and seven New Zealand Amateur championships. GF: $30 AFF, $50 NON.

If it rains, visit the Sarjeant Gallery in Wanganui, one of the finest art galleries in the country.

Marton Golf Club
Web www.marton.nzgolf.net
Phone 06 327 6595
Email marton@golf.co.nz

Castlecliff Golf Club
Web www.castlecliffgolfclub.org.nz
Phone 06 344 4554
Email enquiries@castlecliffgolfclub.org.nz

Wanganui Golf Club
Web www.wanganuigolfclub.co.nz
Phone 06 349 0559
Email manager@wanganuigolfclub.co.nz

Simon Owen
See **Local Heroes**, *page 218*

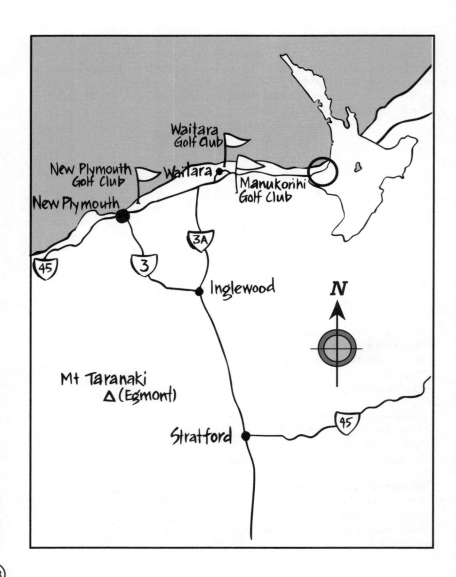

New Plymouth North

The conditions for playing golf in Taranaki are often decided by the mountain. If Mt Taranaki is in a bad mood and blowing wind, only the strong mad-keen survive. But if you're in New Plymouth on one of those perfectly calm, sunny Taranaki days when the sky is rich blue and the broken-tooth cap of the mountain is, with luck, in full view and covered with a bit of snow, then it really doesn't matter where you play golf, you will have a great day out . . . because the mountain says so.

One way to get started is to drive 10 minutes north on State Highway 3 to Waitara. Make the turn-off into town, and through the town and across the bridge over the Waitara River you'll find the **Waitara Golf Club** at the end of Mouatt Street.

From Marton to Castlecliff to Waitara: another set of three, each a terrific little links on the west coast. Waitara is only 4720 metres long from the back tees, which is why it's a good place to begin a golf trip to Taranaki. It's not hilly yet it's by the sea and though the rough can be rough and sand is sand no matter where it lies, this course is more fun than difficult.

The 5th hole here may be the signature as well as a place where the John Dalys among us can leave their mark. At only 385 metres long for men, 362 metres for women, it might be the shortest par-5 in the country. Moreover, it's possible to step to the tee here and feel the wind at your back.

Yet this is a dogleg with OB on the left, so cutting the corner not only means running the risk of going too far left, it means getting around or over a big pine tree. The 5th is, however, the only hole of its kind on the course for men. Women have the luxury of three short par-5s to choose from.

The course plays next to the Tasman Sea but apart from teaming up with the mountain to test your willpower, it never comes into play. The green at the par-4 15th hole and the tee at the par-4 16th are as close as you'll get. Tip: Here, as with all links on the west coast, to score well means being mindful of where the ball rests in relation to your feet. If you don't know, see your nearest pro before playing these courses, as all have fairways with little or no even playing field.

It must have been one of those perfectly still Taranaki days when one of the top senior players in the country, Murray Martin, a member here, set the course record with a sizzling 59. Say 'g'day' to Bill, who told me his favourite hole was the 19th. GF: $15 for all.

If the mountain is grumpy, begin this trip at the **Manukorihi Golf Club** instead. Drive further north on SH3 across the Waitara River and at the top of the hill you'll see the sign to the golf club.

This course is more sheltered from prevailing southerlies and it's easier walking, if only because you're not walking over sand.

As if to give players the option of playing 6, 12 or all 18 holes, Manukorihi plays like a combination of three 6-hole courses where the 6th, 12th, and 18th holes finish near the clubhouse. The tree-lined fairways are wide enough here to keep even high handicappers in play. There's not a single water hazard in sight and because the bunkers are few and far between the course is friendly. Judging from the foursome I came across, the members are too.

That said, do not go long on the par-3 11th hole. Do that and you run the risk of ending up in a nicely planted flower bed and some members do not like seeing their rhododendrons and camellias knocked around by flying golf balls or, worse, stepped on by players looking for their ball. GF: $15 AFF, $20 NON.

Now that you're feeling more in-the-groove after two days on the coast, treat yourself to one of the finest golf courses in the country: Ngamotu Links, formally known as the **New Plymouth Golf Club**. Just about any listing of New Zealand's best courses includes Ngamotu for good reason: the seaside layout is not a links, so it's unique in that way, and the fairways and greens are perpetually in such good condition that visitors (and it gets its fair share) will invariably compare this course with resort courses they have known.

The course is located down what's almost a hidden drive directly off State Highway 3, minutes north of New Plymouth. If you drive through Bell Block you've gone too far.

In the 1920s Ngamotu was the home club of Phil Grey, the best left-handed golfer in New Zealand before Bob Charles. The club is more than a hundred years old and since the 1930s it has hosted numerous national championships, including four New Zealand Opens. US PGA Tour professional, Phil Tataurangi, won the 1993 New Zealand Amateur title here. The club's current touring pro,

Grant Moorhead, holds the course record of 64.

Ngamotu has terrific views of the Tasman Sea in one direction and the mountain in another. On the front nine the par-3 6th hole is the signature hole. It's a picturesque little gem (which is why a lot of photos have been taken there) that tees off from an elevated tee down to a good-sized green. The only catch is there's an equally huge pond in front of the green and bunkers on each side.

On the back nine, the par-3 14h hole is only 116 metres long from the white tees. It has one of the best sea views on the golf course, only you might pay a price for that as it can play directly into the face of a stiff westerly. I'm sure visitors from overseas, who often turn up here to play, find it hard to comprehend how such a fine course can charge so little for green fees. GF: $30 AFF, $60 NON.

Waitara Golf Club
Phone 06 754 8923
Email waitara@golf.co.nz

Manukorihi Golf Club
Phone 06 754 7497
Email manukorihi@golf.co.nz

New Plymouth Golf Club
Web www.golfer.co.nz
Phone 06 755 1349
Email npgc@paradise.net.nz

New Plymouth North

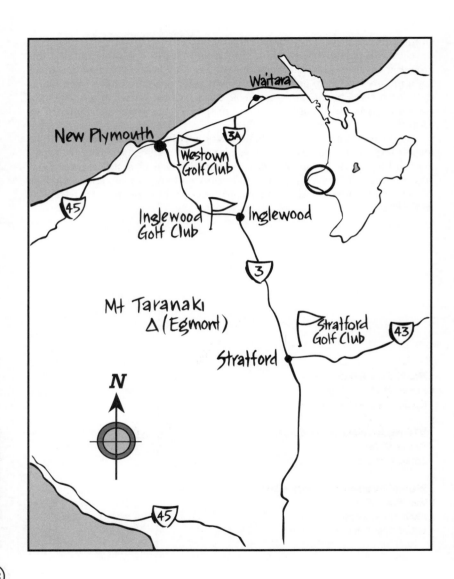

Taranaki Country

From New Plymouth it's less than an hour's drive south on State Highway 3 to Stratford, a town named with Shakespeare's birthplace in mind, and one that claims to have the only Glockenspiel clock tower in the country, itself Shakespearean in every way. The Glockenspiel, by the way, plays three times a day.

From the clock tower you're not far from the **Stratford Golf Club**, a course that, in spite of being a lovely parklands course with row upon row of trees, has fairways so wide even players who tend to slice the ball off the tee are reprieved. You'll find the course just north of town off State Highway 3 at the very end of Pembroke Road.

Of course (pun intended) that's not always the case. But this course is only 5486 metres from the white tees and friendlier still because some of the greens at Stratford are ballroom dance-floors and though there are bunkers at just about every hole, the course is especially nice to big hitters. The fairways are not only wide, they are straight. Here distance off the tee rather than finesse around the green is the key to scoring well. Take the 6th hole, the Number 1 Stroke hole, for example. At 492 metres from the white tees, it's an average-length par-5. But it's dead straight, more or less.

The club turned 100 years old in 2006. GF: $20 AFF, $25 NON.

After golf try Yummy's (I'm not making that up) in town for a sandwich. If you plan to stay overnight in 'the Heart of Taranaki', as the town bills itself, you may want to take a sunset drive up the mountain to Egmont National Park. The road up is opposite the golf club on State Highway 3.

Inglewood, once known as Moatown, does not have a cool clock tower but it does have New Zealand's only toy museum. Play the **Inglewood Golf Club** the next day. Inglewood is no more than a 15-minute drive south from New Plymouth on State Highway 3. Just north of town turn right onto Lepper Road Upper and you'll find it.

Where the course at Stratford is relatively flat, fat, and friendly, perhaps it's the location of this course, closer to the mountain, that makes it far less predictable. The fairways and greens here come with a host of hidden tricks, compensation perhaps for the fact that at 4600 metres from the white tees, this is one of the shortest courses you'll ever play. But like all things short, it won't hit you over the head but it will rear up and bite you in the arse.

The landscape here has nips and tucks and sand traps and elevated greens and trees (of course, always trees) to force you to think (for a change) about each and every shot. A stream comes into play on at least five holes, though in most cases not enough to frighten anyone who is truly mad-keen.

The par-3 17th hole here is a terrific golf hole: short and picture perfect, and if you're looking for a Gainsborough-like vision of the English countryside you'll find it here. Why? Because that's what the people who built this botanical garden had in mind when they built it. Almost all golf courses in Taranaki have views of the mountain, but Inglewood can make a good case for having the best. Native trees form a perfect frame for the mountain at the par-4 15th hole, where you should have your camera ready. GF: $20 AFF, $25 NON.

After golf at Inglewood, try the Kauri Cottage Café up the mountain at Egmont Village for a late lunch.

From New Plymouth drive south the next morning on SH3 for 10 minutes to Mangorei Road, where you'll find the **Westown Golf Club**. The clubhouse sits on a hill overlooking the course. Like the other two courses you've played on this trip, Westown is beautifully maintained with terrific views of Mt Taranaki and though it's close to New Plymouth, it feels so in-the-country you'd never guess there was a city so close by. Craig Owen, one of the well-known Owen brothers originally from Wanganui and one of the top Senior Tour professionals in this part of the world, is the manager here.

Westown is scenic, but it isn't easy. The front nine concludes with (from the blue tees) a 378-metre par-4 dogleg right, uphill to a split-level green. A monster drive of about 250 metres from the back tees is needed to clear the turn for a clear second shot to the green. For many, the approach shot here is either a long-iron or, on some days, a fairway wood — and you're still not home.

Out the back the par-3 14th hole, called 'Mae West', is both beautiful and tough. It plays across a gully to an elevated green that, as members like to say, begs you to 'Come up and see me sometime'.

The signature, however, is the par-4 15th hole, called 'The Wrecker', because its two gullies and small elevated green with a bunker on the left can wreck what has otherwise been a decent round of golf. GF: $25 AFF, $30 NON.

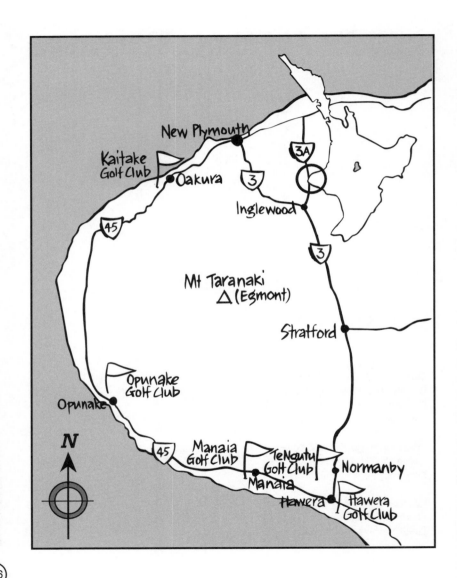

Surf Highway

Drive along the south Taranaki coast and golf courses, like the surf, come in waves. This is the only trip in this book with five courses, because it wasn't fair to leave one or two out. With that in mind, I leave it to you to make the cut.

From New Plymouth this trip makes its first stop at the **Kaitake Golf Club** in Oakura, about 20 minutes south on State Highway 45. Oakura is a small coastal settlement with its own micro-climate because it's sheltered from the prevailing southerlies by the mountain and the Kaitake Range. When a southerly moves in, Kaitake can be playable when other courses in Taranaki are more like an expedition than a game. If the westerly turns up, however, Kaitake gets it right in the belly.

The short par-4 5th hole here is only 280 metres long for men and women alike, but it's one of the sharpest doglegs in the world. The club is being too folksy calling this hole simply: 'Around the Bend'. But for most of us, short par-4s, whether they have a radical dogleg in them or not, are what we like to see.

The par-3 9th hole that can be seen from the highway is a neat little par-3, with bunkers and a big sloping green that even at 140 metres from the blue tees seems impossible to miss. But, as always in golf, appearances can be deceptive. Kaitake is a parklands-style golf course and one of the lesser-known Taranaki courses, but it has plenty of character and you get a free drop should your ball land in a tractor track. GF: $15 AFF, $20 NON.

State Highway 45 between New Plymouth and Hawera is, in tourism-speak, the 'Surf Highway' because some of the best surfing in the Southern Hemisphere is found along this magnificent coast. Opunake has a surf school.

When the surf's not up, however, drive out to the **Opunake Golf Club** and knock a ball around. The course is on Namu Road off the main highway on the north side of town. On the day of my visit this coast was getting its fair share of wind and wicked-looking white caps were kicking up a fuss on the Tasman Sea.

Still, I found my way through a downpour to the course only to learn that it's short — only 5300 metres long for men, 4800 metres long for women — and that it's probably fun for the whole family if not a course the big hitters would enjoy. The par-3 18th hole, for example, is a straight 120-metre shot for men and women alike, a finishing feel-good hole if there ever was one.

Opunake is a rough track, but when it comes to mad-keen golfers never bet against South Taranaki dairy farmers — for in spite of the utterly miserable weather on the day, the car park was full! GF: $10 for all.

For lunch in Opunake try the Sugar Juice Café or Muzza's Bar & Grill. From Opunake, drive on to Manaia and the **Manaia Golf Club**. There you'll begin to understand what I mean when I say the only problem with calling this coastal road the 'Surf Highway' is this: the name pays more homage to the Beach Boys than it does to the history of South Taranaki.

To gain some understanding of this, when you play here have a peek inside the blockhouse that sits on a former Maori redoubt in the middle of the golf course. The blockhouse is a reconstruction of what was originally a watchtower during the war between Maori and Pakeha in 1880–81. A plaque there reminded me that Parihaka was not far away and that British cadets once stood in a tower similar to this one keeping an eye on the pacifist Maori leader, Te Whiti.

Manaia is a short, sweet country treat with views of surrounding farmland and the Waiokura Stream. The par-3 9th hole plays through a gap in trees and over the stream and the par-5 8th hole and the par-4 10th have that lateral water hazard for the entire length of the fairway. Like all the courses on this trip, beginners can have fun here too. But with that in mind, heed the sign on the entry gate that warns: 'Beware of Golf Balls.' GF: $15 AFF, $20 NON.

Historic Hawera is only a few minutes further along the road. You'll know you've arrived when you see the Water Tower, constructed between 1912 and 1914 and with an interesting story of its own. According to the brochure from the information centre, 'Te Hawera' means 'the burnt place', a reference to a feud between two Maori tribes that left the village, as it was then, burned to the ground. And now that you've played two courses already on this trip, you may be 'on fire' too. Drive north from town a few minutes on State Highway 3, make the turn at the hotel in Normanby (there is only one) and you'll find the **Te Ngutu Golf Club**.

Te Ngutu has immaculate greens. The most-talked about hole on the course is the par-3 11th, which is not long but it is down. The green is about 30 metres below the hole. Talk about a drop shot. The club has built a new 6th hole recently that may replace the 11th as the signature hole, for this is also a par-3 — but one that plays from a plateau tee to a plateau green. Here you either hit the green or die . . . just kidding. The par-5 5th hole may be the only golf hole in New Zealand with the green built on top of a redoubt. GF: $20 for all.

Finally, as a test to see just how mad-keen you really are, the **Hawera Golf Club** is a links course — sand dunes, salty air, the constant sea breeze — at the end of Fairfield Road. Take State Highway 3 to the south end of town and turn right at the fire station.

This links course, 5565 metres long from the men's tee, 5150 metres from the women's tee, is relatively flat and easy to get around on foot. It's partly sheltered by rows of mature pohutukawa that when in bloom (I was too early for that) no doubt make this course especially attractive to play.

Score a hole-in-one here on the par-3 10th hole and you might win a $200 voucher from Zodiac Signs (who made the sign). GF: $15 for all.

The Avon Lodge or the Rembrandt Motel back out on the main road may suit for overnight. If it rains use your golf umbrella and take the walking tour of Historic Hawera, then visit the Tawhiti Museum.

Kaitake Golf Club
Phone 06 752 7665
Email kaitake@golf.co.nz

Opunake Golf Club
Phone 06 761 8070
Email opunake@paradise.net.nz

Manaia Golf Club
Phone 06 274 8325
Email manaia@golf.co.nz

Te Ngutu Golf Club
Phone 06 272 8039
Email tengutu@golf.co.nz

Hawera Golf Club
Phone 06 278 5828

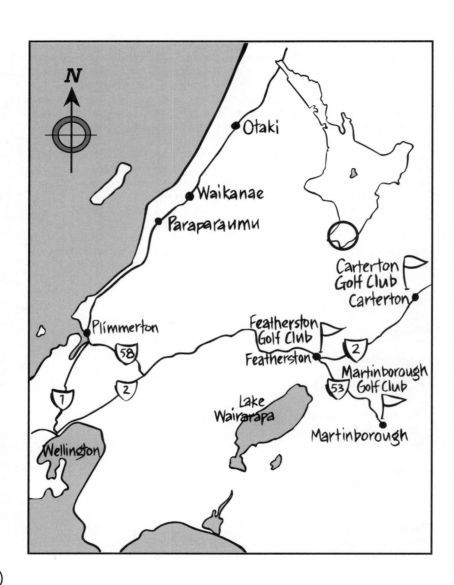

Wairarapa South

Apart from local residents — farmers and wine-makers mainly — the majority of golf roadies to the Wairarapa come from Wellington. Or should I say 'come over' from Wellington, because from that direction the drive takes you over the Rimutaka Range.

The drive from the capital to Featherston takes about an hour. Featherston produces a very good free guide book to 'Featherston Country' that's full of information on where to stay and eat. Call in at the visitor information centre on Fitzherbert Street when you arrive.

The **Featherston Golf Club** is off Western Lake Road about five minutes from town. Watch for the club sign where you'll turn left. Club president Cath Berry was watering the garden around the clubhouse when I arrived. Tee bookings weren't necessary, she said. People here just roll up and play any time they like.

Featherston has no bunkers but it does have a drain that cuts across the course and comes into play on the back nine. The course's mid-sized circular (more or less) greens were in good condition, though slow on the day simply because they had not been mowed in a day or two. But none of this is why you should play here.

You play Featherston because you want to tell your grandchildren that one day you played on the flattest golf course on earth. If the Flat Earth Society is still looking for evidence — maybe a conference venue — then the Featherston Golf Club is perfect. Another joke: This course is so flat it has no slope rating.

Okay, so there's a small knoll here and there. The par-4 4th hole is not long but your tee shot has to find its way to the turn of a dogleg right and if your second shot comes up short, your ball can wind up in the drain.

Three of the back nine holes play across the drain, but my guess is the drain does not cause regulars here as much grief as the boundary fence that's OB. The signature hole here is the par-3 5th hole that, at 203 metres long *from the ladies tee*, is the longest par-3 in the Wairarapa.

Warning: If you haven't paid your green fees you will be tracked down by a black-and-white Mini with a flashing red light on top. That'll be the club 'police car' and it's worth a photo. GF: $15 for all.

It's about a 15-minute drive from Featherston to the charming village square in Martinborough where, for all the World War I and World War II memorials around the country, you'll find one here dedicated to the Boer War. The more recent Martinborough story, however, is wine.

Martinborough now boasts about 40 wineries, so it shouldn't surprise you to find the **Martinborough Golf Club** bordered by vineyards and a new subdivision. In fact, if you slice your tee shot too far right on the par-4 3rd hole your ball can end up across the road in the Pencarrow vineyard of Palliser Estate Wines.

The golf course, however, is not about vineyards so much as it's about trees. All golf courses have trees, of course. For most country courses trees shape the fairways in ways that do little else but cause havoc and frustration. Martinborough is different because the trees here are not restrictive rows of boring old pine. Instead, there are 30 different varieties of oak, a comprehensive collection of natives, and my favourite: a rare 'strawberry tree' right in the fairway at the par-4 14th hole. The hole is only 285 metres long from the white tees so for big hitters it should be open-and-shut (okay, for big hitters who are lawyers). But the strawberry tree, so-called because its fruit looks a bit like a strawberry, is a small obstacle best avoided by playing left.

Trees are the main characters in the plot at the par-4 10th hole too, only in this case it's a boring old pine with big furry branches hanging out to produce an exceptionally narrow gap for an approach to the green. On the day of my visit one of the branches was broken off and hanging limp. It was easy enough to imagine an angry member trying to pull it down. Whoever it was, they had my support. GF: $20 AFF, $30 NON.

We checked into the modest Martinborough Motel because it was the last place in town with a vacancy. The demand for accommodation here can be greater than the supply, so readers are encouraged to book. As if to drown my sorrows for the bogey on the 3rd hole, I shouted a bottle of the 2003 Palliser Estate Pencarrow Pinot Noir at the Martinborough Hotel that night.

We drove a back road (Ponatahi Road) over to Carterton the next day. Carterton is the 'Gateway to the Tararuas'. The **Carterton Golf Club** may be the only non-resort course in the country that produces its own course guide. It has a sketch of each hole and shows the distances and layouts of each. In some instances it even tells you the names of significant trees too — although I know a 'Big Pine' when I see one.

The guide does not, however, identify the trees at the signature hole. The par-3 12th has totara trees standing tall directly between the tee and the green. Because it's impossible to hit through them, players either loft a shot over them, in which case you then stoop to see where your shot ends up, or you do as some older members of the club do: hit the ball along the ground and roll it *beneath* the trees.

Less quirky, water in the form of traditional irrigation ditches common to farms in the region comes into play on the 17th and 18th holes. The 18th is a par-5 with H^2O (as the guide says) in front of the green forcing players to choose between laying-up with their second shot or not. The hole is 485 metres long so even for big hitters the smart play is to lay-up. After all, you never can tell what you'll find in a drainage ditch. GF: $20 AFF, $30 NON.

If it rains, visit the Carterton Paua Shell Factory. Go in September and you can take in the Daffodil Carnival.

Featherston Golf Club
Phone 06 308 9266
Email featherston@golf.co.nz

Martinborough Golf Club
Phone 06 306 9266
Email martinborough@golf.co.nz

Carterton Golf Club
Web www.cartertongolf.co.nz
Phone 06 379 8457
Email clubhouse@cartertongolfclub.co.nz

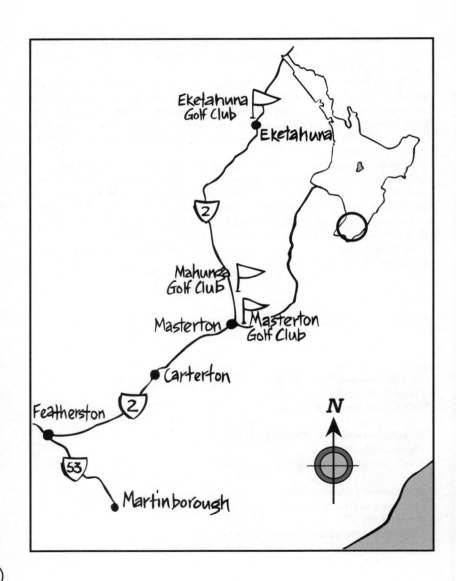

Wairarapa North

Masterton is home to the Golden Shears international shearing competition in March and, accordingly, visitors can learn everything they've always wanted to know about sheep farming at the Shear Discovery Centre. It's also where Sir Bob Charles first played golf. As a teenager Sir Bob played at the **Masterton Golf Club**.

The club, located up the hill on the corner of Manuka Street and Boltons Road, was founded in 1899. Winning the New Zealand Open four times and the British Open once is probably enough to justify re-naming the club lounge The Bob Charles Lounge. One of his original golf bags hangs like an artefact on the clubhouse wall.

'Lansdowne', as the Masterton course is also known, plays along ridges and over rolling hills high above town so the view in places is exceptionally panoramic. For anyone seeking a viewing platform to check out Masterton and the Wairarapa valley, they could do no better than the tee of the par-3 11th hole. Scoring par there, however, is another matter. The course plays over hills and down through gullies and in places the drop-off around greens is extreme. The 11th green provides a great view of the territory but once you tee off, if you come up short and on the right, your ball will bound down a slope so steep someone may have to throw you a rope to pull you back up.

Ditto the par-3 13th hole that has an extremely steep drop off the left shoulder of a long, narrow green that slopes from back to front. Push your tee shot too far right (as I did) and you can wind up in hilly rough or worse, in a small drainage ditch (as I did).

The course dries out in summer. It's the downside of not having fairway irrigation and being situated on a hill. So summer golf here is quite a lot different from winter golf, where your tee shot is less likely to bounce off fairways that often slope left or right. GF: $20 AFF, $30 NON.

The flash place to stay in Masterton is the Copthorne Solway Park Hotel —

à la carte dining, indoor and outdoor pools, a spa and gymnasium, tennis courts, solarium, even a golf driving range. Try Café Cecille for lunch or dinner.

But long before the Copthorne arrived here there was the Kaikokirikiri Pa, the stronghold of the great Wairapapa chief, Retimana Te Korou. The pa remains in its earthen form today at the **Mahunga Golf Club**. You'll see it as you walk from the 10th green to the 11th tee. The 10th, by the way, is a par-3 — 181 metres long from the men's tee, 149 metres long from the women's tee. The 11th is a flat-out par-5, 443 metres long for men, 414 metres for women.

The opening hole here is a par-4, 280 metres long for men and women (no sexism here). It has a creek running along the entire left flank of the fairway and a gorgeous giant matai standing next to it looking spooky. A creek cuts across the fairway in front of the green.

Did I say spooky? Mahunga is the only golf course in the country with a ghost. Club legend has it that the ghost is an old Maori man, who appears on the 9th tee and can be heard to say: 'Kaore te pai taua puhi' which means: 'That wasn't a good shot'.

Hey, I just report these things.

Some say the signature hole here is the par-5 14th that's optimistically called 'Never Despair'. Here, the stream, like a pesky fly that won't leave you alone, creeps across the fairway in front of the green, naturally forcing players to either lay-up or go for it in two. The last three players who tried to go for the green in two, only to end up in the creek, died. Okay, so I made that up. GF: $20 for all.

Drive north on the third day to Eketahuna, a town that most consider southern Hawke's Bay not the Wairarapa. But Eketahuna is only a short drive from Masterton and once you've seen this throw-back gem of a country track it won't matter where you are exactly.

The **Eketahuna Golf Club**, located at the north end of town, is a bucolic course where sheep graze quietly and the greens have electric fences around them to keep the sheep in their place. Once, most country courses grazed sheep. It made economic sense (see 'Kapiti Coast'). But few courses follow this practice today, so teeing off at Eketahuna and playing among sheep is, in that way, like going back in time. The only other course in this book with sheep still grazing on it is at Raglan (see 'Hamilton West'). Here, if your ball strikes a wire fence encircling a green, tough luck. You play the ball where it lies.

Eketahuna is only 5300 metres long for men, 5100 metres for women. As a short but scenic course, and the final stop on this long weekend, mad-keen golfers should go home feeling good about their game.

This course calls for some good shot-making as you would expect from a 'target' course. Take the opening hole, for example. It's a par-4 and only 280 metres long for both men and women, but it has a sharp dogleg right around a giant macrocarpa. This tree has branches sticking out like big nets to catch the tee shots of fools who believe they can cut the corner and reach the green in one.

Tip: Unless your name is Tiger Woods use an iron or fairway wood off the first tee here. Play around the big tree, not through it. Once you round the corner of the first hole, however, no matter where your ball lies, take a moment to enjoy the scenery for this course is shaped in part by the Makakahi River and its stunning sandstone cliffs. The par-3 10th hole plays in the gorge above the river and below the cliffs. Your shot has to negotiate two small trees that act as a gateway to a small green that drops off sharply at the back.

The par-4 11th hole is called 'Double Gap' because it zigzags (some would call this a modest double dogleg) between two groves of more big macrocarpa with overhanging limbs. Your tee shot doesn't have to be long, but it does have to be in the right position (on the left) to give you any chance of a clear approach shot to the green.

The greens at Eketahuna are in excellent condition and the sheep make sure the fairways are kept down. Eketahuna is one of the seven courses that host the Wairarapa Festival of Golf each February — a good time to go. The course record of 63 was set by Manawatu's Tim Wilkinson in January 2005. GF: $15 for all.

Masterton Golf Club
Web www.mastergolf.org.nz
Phone 06 377 4984
Email enquiries@mastergolf.co.nz

Mahunga Golf Club
Phone 06 377 4990
Email mahunga@golf.co.nz

Eketahuna Golf Club
Phone 06 375 8143
Email eketahuna@golf.co.nz

Sir Bob Charles
See **Local Heroes**, page 218

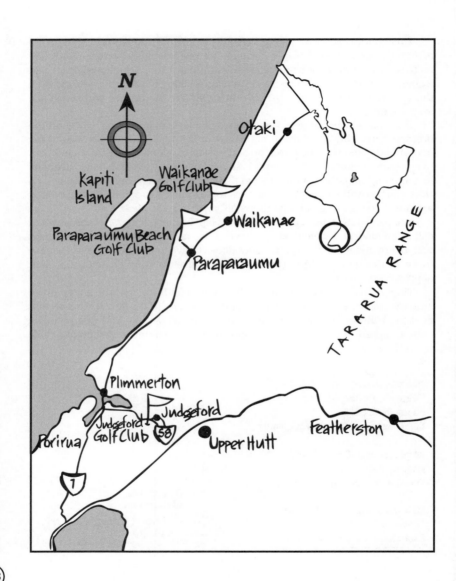

Kapiti Coast

The Kapiti Coast is named for the mighty Kapiti Island that from this shoreline can, on some days, appear close enough to touch. This coastal strip, starting at Paekakariki (assuming you're driving north from Wellington), is sometimes called 'the nature coast' for a good reason: it's a hive of coastal walks along the shore and through native bush and formal gardens.

Nature aside, you'll get plenty of bush and sea to play with if you come here to play golf. Make your first stop at the **Judgeford Golf Club** on State Highway 58 linking this coast to the Hutt Valley. You can't miss the course because the highway runs through it. Twelve holes are on one side of the road, the clubhouse side, and six are on the other.

Judgeford has the most difficult opening hole in the world. This par-4 1st hole is 330 metres long for men and women alike and while that's not especially long across the flat (a long-drive champion would reach the green in a single swift blow), this hole plays up a hill and around a corner, through a gap and over a stream to an extremely elevated green.

Starting your day with a par here is worth a certificate. The stream is so tight on the right it's possible, indeed likely, that your first shot of the day will wind up there and OB.

The par-3 7th hole features a vertical drop from tee to green of about 45 degrees to a small green with OB on the left and a creek (a small abyss) at the back. The layout here can be mean but the greens are among the best you'll ever play on. The club's annual amateur match-play tournament, the Steinlager Summer Cup, was won in its inaugural year (1992) by none other than (Sir) Michael Campbell.

From Judgeford make the drive over Paekakariki Hill, stopping along the way for photos. Down at sea level again, the Kapiti Gateway Motel in Waikanae will save you money on green fees if you play their local course or its more famous neighbour at Paraparaumu Beach.

The **Waikanae Golf Club** is a course used for qualifying whenever the New Zealand Open is played at Paraparaumu Beach — which won't be for a few years yet, as the Gulf Harbour Country Club north of Auckland has a temporary lock on that tournament.

Waikanae is also the site of Steve Williams's annual charity tournament. Williams, the long-serving and highly successful caddie for Tiger Woods, is from this area originally, though both this fine links course and its loftier neighbour down the road lay claim to being Williams' official home course. Williams is on record saying his home course is South Head (see 'Harbour and Surf').

If you've never had a hole-in-one or you lie awake at night dreaming of another, play the par-3 8th hole at Waikanae. It's an elevated tee shot across a ravine to a plateau-green that has a steep gully at the back. Here you find the green from the tee or suffer the consequences. It appears like a bear in the woods, but club general manager Blair Coburn told me this hole produces as many as 15 holes-in-one each year. So *that's* why this club, with 900 members, is the biggest on the Kapiti Coast.

The par-4 9th hole tests your accuracy off the tee over a narrow saddle to a 'blind' fairway, but the par-4 13th hole may be the signature. Take a moment here to stand on the blue tee and you'll see what I mean. It plays across a wetland of toi toi, flax, cabbage trees, and, visible from the other tees only, a stream. It's a dogleg left and one of the best holes in this region.

Two ponds split the fairway of the par-4 15th. They're not deep, but should your ball wind up there watch out for the 'crocodile'. GF: $25 AFF, $35 NON.

For Day Three, book your tee time at **Paraparaumu Beach Golf Club**, a course many consider to be the best links in New Zealand. This seaside gem was designed by Alex Russell, an outstanding Australian player (he won the 1924 Aussie Open). In time Russell became a partner of famed American course architect, Dr Alister Mackenzie.

Paraparaumu has hosted the New Zealand Open 12 times. The course record is 62, mutually held by Sir Bob Charles, the Englishman Maurice Bembridge, and Australian Paul Gow. I hope that for most readers that's a point of trivia only, not a life-goal, because shooting any score less than 70 here is an exceptional feat.

This is not an easy course and the slope rating of 124 from the white tees doesn't begin to tell the story. Some golf courses demand that players be long off the tee if they want to score well. Being long off the tee here will help you score well too, but it's not the 'long game' that counts here so much as the 'short game'.

Paraparaumu wasn't designed to be a 'target' course, but with the introduction of titanium drivers and solid-core balls it's become that. Tiger Woods made his only appearance in New Zealand here, at the Open in 2002, and my guess is he left his driver in the bag most of the time because here touch and finesse around the green matter more than distance off the tee.

Paraparaumu is a terrific Old World-style course with deep, classic pot bunkers, rolling greens, and severe greenside slopes that can deflate the ego in an instant. The greens are very quick. Someone playing the course for the first time might take the entire front nine to find the right speed and putting stroke, if they ever do.

This course has at least two of the best par-3s in the country. The 14th plays from tee to green over a deep ravine, and the 16th plays to a long, narrow green with a hill on the left and a steep shoulder drop-off on the right.

The par-4 17th hole is one of the best par-4s in the country. It's not strictly a dogleg right, but to avoid the risk of winding up in one of the two high dunes that cut across the fairway, that's how it should be played — left to right. Staying right off the tee brings two greenside bunkers into play.

Look for the marked spot on the 18th fairway where Grant Waite scored a sensational albatross on the second day (not the final day as legend has it) and went on to win the 1992 New Zealand Open. GF: $45 AFF, $60 NON.

Judgeford Golf Club
Web www.judgefordgolf.co.nz
Phone 04 235 7633
Email webmaster@judgefordgolf.co.nz

Waikanae Golf Club
Web www.waikanaegolfclub.co.nz
Phone 04 293 6399
Email waikanae@golf.co.nz

Paraparaumu Beach Golf Club
Web www.paraparaumubeachgolfclub.co.nz
Phone 04 902 8200
Email office@paraparaumubeachgolfclub.co.nz

Kapiti Coast

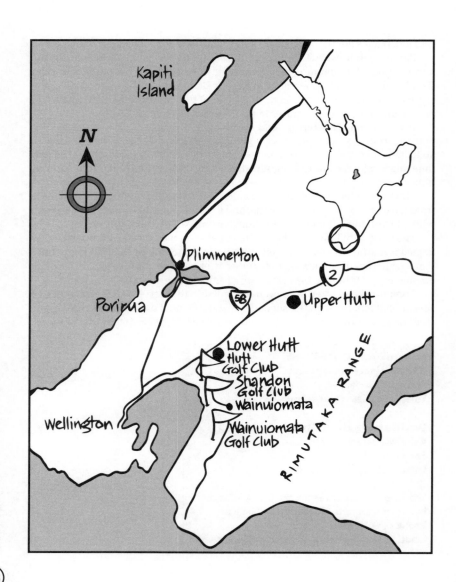

Lower Hutt

Wainuiomata, a working-class, state-housing town on the other side of the hill, is separated from the mainstream in more ways than one. But don't let that put you off playing golf at the Wainuiomata Golf Club, one of the most pleasant places to play in the entire Wellington region.

Follow the road over the hill and down through town. Swing right onto Coast Road and you'll find the golf course on your right. You'll see it first through a grove of eucalyptus that, like a natural curtain, separates the golf course from the road.

The first green (though not the 1st hole) you're likely to see as you drive in here will be on your immediate left. It's the 13th hole, a strip of land that was once a horse paddock, that's now one of the best par-3s in the region.

To fully appreciate that, play it from the back tee, the only tee that's elevated enough to see the hole in perspective. It plays over wetlands to a rolling green with four bunkers and the eucalyptus grove for a backdrop.

Wainuiomata, the only course in New Zealand managed by women, has built four new greens in recent years and under the direction of operations manager, Donna Fifield, and business manager, Raewyn Hanson, more improvements are likely.

The Wainui River flows through the course and adds considerable charm to this parklands-style course that, for as close to the Hutt Valley as it is, feels remote. The river has cut its way through the property over the years leaving the landscape uneven, so the course plays on a higher — though still flat — plain at the back. Water comes into play on at least six holes, but the signature hole has no water at all.

At 194 metres from the white tees, the 4th hole may be the shortest par-4 in New Zealand golf. But it plays over a deep ravine to a narrow landing area with an extremely steep drop-off on the right. To avoid going right, some players will use a fairway wood or even an iron off this tee and lay-up, leaving them in a better position to approach a green that's tucked left slightly behind trees. Or you can use the driver and go straight at the green and risk ending up in the trees on the left or down in the abyss on the right. It's one of those holes you play mentally, not physically.

But that short, 'target' hole is the exception here, for playing Wainuiomata well means generally being long off the tee. Big hitters should score well here because the course is only 5500 metres long (off the white tees) and the tree-lined fairways here are wide and friendly. GF: $20 AFF, $25 NON weekdays; $25 AFF, $35 NON weekends.

If only the Hutt Valley had as many options for accommodation as it has cafés on Jackson Street. The Hutt is not perceived as a place someone might want to go on holiday, so maybe that's why it has hardly any places to stay. Playing golf here over a long weekend might mean commuting each day from Wellington, although we found the Riddiford Hotel on Knights Road in Lower Hutt just fine. The hotel is there, it seems, to cater primarily to visitors from China. As someone who has played golf there, it was like old times for me.

Wherever you choose to spend the night, play the **Shandon Golf Club** on Day Two. Shandon plays between the Hutt River and one of its tributaries, but unless you hit an especially bad shot these rivers do not come into play. To find the course turn left off Waione Street onto Jessie Street.

The water hazards at Shandon are internal, like the par-5 17th hole or the par-3 18th where water near and in front of the green might unnerve some players. Of course, the decision at the 17th, as it is with any par-5 with water close to the green, is whether to go for it in two or not.

Hitting the ball long here is not as important as playing smart. Big hitters will be tempted to unleash their fury off the tee at the par-4 1st hole, for example. It's a slight dogleg left around trees, more suited to a fairway wood or a long-iron off the tee. Go too long off the tee here and you'll wind up in Nottingham Forest, so to speak.

Likewise, the par-5 10th hole is only 411 metres for men and women, but it bends around to the left. Here, pulling the driver out with the aim of reaching the green in two is a sure way of winding up among trees.

This course is 5600 metres long for men, 5250 metres long for women, but the fairways are uneven with significant mounds and gullies. Its sprawling greens are some of the best in the region. Because the course is located in an industrial zone and bordered by the river, it's like a quiet oasis removed from the bustle all around. GF: $35 AFF, $40 NON midweek; $40 AFF, $50 NON weekends.

The pearl of this trip, however, must be the **Hutt Golf Club**. Follow High Street north through Lower Hutt and you'll soon see the sign pointing left on Military Road. Hutt is the oldest golf club in the North Island. Formed by a Scotsman (who else?) named David Howden in 1892, the course was first designed by Commander John Harris and later tweaked by Michael Wolveridge, of the design team that created Wairakei International in Taupo.

The fairways here are wide enough that even those of us who still can't hit the ball straight can keep the ball in play. It's what happens after that that matters most here. The par-4 6th hole is 343 metres long off the white tees. It's easy enough to find the fairway off the tee, but then your second shot is to a small green with two big, smiling bunkers on the right and a sharp drop-off beyond. Likewise, the par-4 9th hole is straightforward enough but your second shot has to negotiate multiple fairway bunkers.

Hutt is the kind of golf course where players could hit every fairway in regulation and still not score well. The signature hole might be the sweet-looking par-3 18th. It's called 'Waterloo' and though it's only 98 metres long it plays over a pond to a *three-tiered* green, flanked by three bunkers on the sides and a fourth at the back. It's one of the best par-3s in the country and when you finish your round take time to enjoy a snack on the classy clubhouse deck. GF: $50 AFF, $65 NON.

Wainuiomata Golf Club
Web www.wainuigolf.co.nz
Phone 04 564 7746
Email wainuigolf@xtra.co.nz

Shandon Golf Club
Web www.shandongolf.co.nz
Phone 04 939 6308
Email shandon@golf.co.nz

Hutt Golf Club
Web www.huttgolfclub.co.nz
Phone 04 546 4722
Email admin@huttgolfclub.org.nz

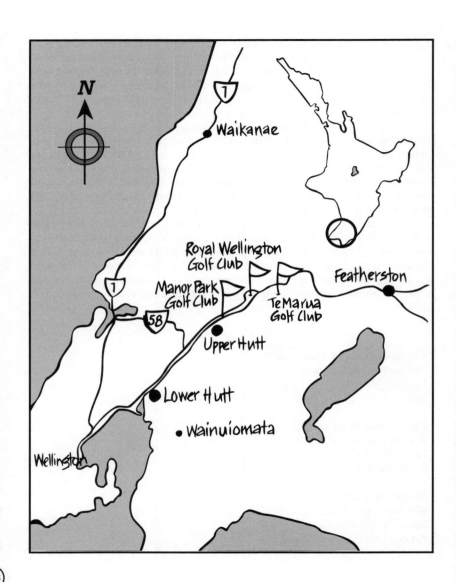

the Mad Keen Golfer's Road Trip

Upper Hutt

Upper Hutt is the location for some scenes in *Lord of the Rings* (for example, Helms Deep and Isengard) and it's also where you'll find three fine golf courses, one with a royal take of its own. There's no Rivendell or Hobbit Village to stay in overnight, but you might try the Hawk's Inn on Ferguson Drive close to Upper Hutt City or the new Silverstream Retreat, a motel that overlooks the Hutt River and the first stop on this long weekend of golf: the **Manor Park Golf Club**.

Manor Park is something of a golf factory. Under the direction of golf coach Mal Tongue and his staff, the club has produced some of New Zealand's best players, foremost being Michael Campbell, winner of the 2005 US Open.

Campbell began playing golf at that now historic 9-hole course in Titahi Bay. He joined Manor Park at the age of 14. Other top Kiwi professionals hatched here are European Tour players Lynnette Brooky, Stephen Scahill and Gareth Paddison.

Manor Park is the longest course in Wellington. It has to be to conform to the narrow strip of land it's laid out on, one that's shaped by the fickle Hutt River on one side and State Highway 2 on the other. To find it simply take the Manor Park exit off the motorway and turn left onto Golf Road. Heads up when you walk from the car park to the clubhouse, however, because the footpath intersects two fairways.

The course has a small stream running across three holes on the front nine, but for most players it's only at the par-4 3rd hole where it comes into play. Here, players have to decide whether to lay-up or try to drive over the water that's about 200 metres from the blue tee. It's common to see men (not women) drive the water and leave themselves with an easy pitch shot to the green. For the most part, the stream is not a hazard so much as an attractive addition to the look of the golf course. Stone bridges add a nice Old World touch.

Dylan Lindstrom, one of the latest crop of young guns playing here, brought it to my attention that the last six holes on the front nine are unique in that there is no par-4, only three par-3s and three par-5s. If it's true (and I have yet to see the evidence) that the average golfer scores better on par-3s and par-5s, then the front nine at Manor Park should make even the 18-handicapper feel like Michael Campbell.

Still, the general rule here is to score well, as even on par-3s and par-5s players must hit the ball long and straight. The par-3 7th is 190 metres long from the men's tee, 170 metres from the women's tee. If you're not long and straight here you may wish you had taken up mini-golf instead. GF: $25 AFF, $35 NON weekdays; $35 AFF, $45 NON weekends.

Further along the road and on the other side of the river at Heretaunga is one of the finest golf courses in the world, according to Prince Andrew. He played here in 1998 and again in 2004. On the 250th anniversary of the Royal & Ancient at St Andrews he bestowed the course with a royal title.

The **Royal Wellington Golf Club** is among the most famous golf courses in the country as much for its history and tradition as for the consistently immaculate condition of the course itself. The club's director of golf, Jack Oliver, showed me a photograph taken in 1895 when the course was built. The giant cabbage tree looming next to the 10th tee today is the same tree in the photograph.

Here in 1954 an unknown 18-year-old bank clerk and amateur golfer identified in the newspapers as 'R. J. Charles' won the New Zealand Open. For Sir Bob, it was just the beginning and for 'Heretaunga', as the club is commonly known, it was just one of many opens and national championships played here over the years.

A signature hole? Try all of them. Guests are advised that while playing with a member is recommended, unaccompanied players are welcome. There are less than a hundred Royal golf clubs in the world but significantly only three have been so honoured since World War II, in part because it's as if every member of the royal family since then except Andrew thought of golf as, well, much ado about nothing.

Bookings are essential and, as the reminder on the website says, 'A smart standard of dress is required. Jeans, tracksuits and tee-shirts are not permitted. For men, white ankle socks are permitted with tailored shorts. For women, shirts must have collars and be tucked into trousers, skirts, or shorts — no more than 6cm above the knee.' GF: with a member $60 AFF, $60 NON; unaccompanied by a member $100 AFF, $150 NON.

On the third day, drive through Upper Hutt to the foot of the Rimutaka Range and the **Te Marua Golf Club**. You'll be nicely surprised to discover one of the most picturesque courses in the region for here, more so than on the two previous days, the Hutt River and a stunning cliff face it has carved out over the years, come into view — and sometimes into play. In fact, to strike the perfect tee shot on the par-4 1st hole, 370 metres long for men, 306 metres for women, is to drive the ball *over* the river.

The first tee here is a great introduction to the golf course because it's the highest point on the course. Water comes into play again at the par-4 8th, only it's not the river — it's a pond waiting to swallow your ball should you push your approach shot too far right.

The fairways at Te Marua are generally wide and friendly, but not flat. The par-5 10th hole is as much fun to play as the opening hole, though not because of the river. It's 466 metres long for men, 382 metres for women. It's a dogleg right that plays from one level to another around and down toward the river and the cliffs *and* through (or around) two giant poplar trees in the middle of the fairway. The par-3 11th hole might be the most scenic, as it directly overlooks the gorge. GF: $20 AFF midweek, $25 AFF weekends; $30 NON all the time.

Manor Park Golf Club
Web www.manorparkgolf.co.nz
Phone 04 563 8558
Email manorpark@xtra.co.nz

Royal Wellington Golf Club
Web www.rwgc.co.nz
Phone 04 528 2640
Email office@rwgc.co.nz

Te Marua Golf Club
Web www.temaruagolfclub.co.nz
Phone 04 526 7020
Email temarua@golf.co.nz

Lynnette Brooky
Michael Campbell
See Local Heroes,
page 219

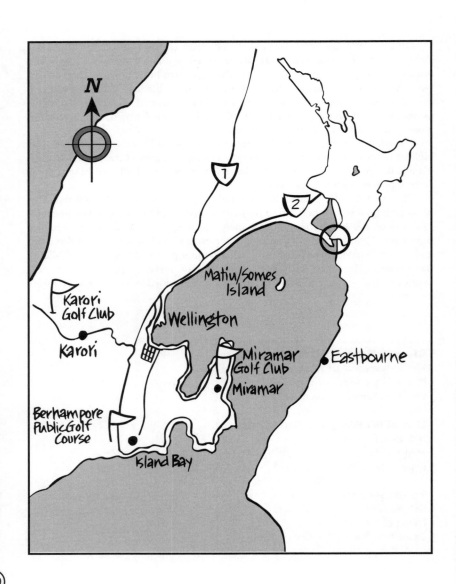

Capital Hills

The Musuem of New Zealand and a reconstructed waterfront with restaurants and bars have made Wellington an especially attractive harbour city. But cities are cities. Golfers looking for a temporary reprieve from Wellington's white noise should head over the hills to the **Karori Golf Club**. Follow the main road through the Karori shops to the AA sign to Makara. Once over the crest of the hill follow the signs to the golf course, located on South Makara Road.

The fairways at Karori are exceptionally tight in places, enough to leave you thinking that trees are okay, it's just too bad they come with branches. Here, like the trees in *Lord of the Rings*, they seem to move in on you, pressing you to hit the ball straight or die.

Karori isn't hilly as much as it's (I'm inventing a word here) slopey. Every hole plays up or down a slope, though not in an extreme way. A creek winds through the course and while it adds character to the landscape, it comes into play on at least five holes.

The signature hole here might be the par-3 2nd with a pine tree right in the bloody middle of the fairway. But you can't get too upset about it because it is without question one of the most noteworthy golf course trees in New Zealand. Stay cool and take your tee shot to one side or the other. Or, as this hole begins from an elevated tee, if you think you are J.B. Holmes, the punk on the US PGA Tour who drives the ball 320 metres, go over it.

Or it may be the 15th hole, a long par-4 for men and an average par-5 for women. From the tee you'll look down to a pond on the right and power lines over the fairway. The combination of the two obstacles can be unsettling to the extent that this can be a surprisingly difficult fairway for players to keep their ball in play, especially surprising when your tee shot strikes a power line.

Or it may be the terrific 16th hole that plays across the creek *twice* — the

Number 1 Stroke hole on the course. GF: $20 AFF, $27 NON weekdays; $27 AFF, $38 NON weekends.

Back in the city, drive out Adelaide Road to Island Bay and you'll come upon the **Berhampore Public Golf Course**, as it's officially known, on your right, adjacent to Wakefield Park. Berhampore is owned by the city but leased to the Mornington Golf Club, which is why the course is called one thing or the other depending on who you talk to. Berhampore/Mornington is a public course, so it's dependent on ratepayers and council funding for upkeep and repair.

This means that, typical of municipal golf courses all over the world, it's nothing flash. Yet, as municipal courses go, this one's not bad.

I found it in reasonably good nick and besides, if there's a single reason for playing here (apart from cheap green fees) it's to brag to others that you have played the hilliest golf course in the world. Come to think of it, if Oreti Sands can hand out certificates (see 'Deep South'), Berhampore/Mornington should too.

Naturally, this is not an easy course to walk but you have no choice. C'mon, you think the council would fund carts? This course is not a test of golf so much as a test of fitness. The reward for the hike, however, is some spectacular views of the city and Cook Strait, and if you haven't guessed by now, personally, I'm into views. They are particularly fine at the par-4 5th and the par-3 7th.

This course is as forgiving as a golf course can be, for it has no water hazards or bunkers. The last five holes play on the opposite side of Adelaide Road, a busy thoroughfare. There's no dedicated bridge or crossing for golfers, it's each man and driver for themselves. Try not to tip your trundler over in the middle of the street.

Across the road, the par-4 14th is more or less flat before the par-4 15th shoots up a hill to a plateau green. At the top, when a northerly is in full force, as club president Ron Fairbairn told me, 'you need your partner to hold you while you putt'. GF: $10 midweek, $15 weekends for all.

Wellington has a zillion options for accommodation and food, so I leave you to do your own research. Make your way on Day Three over to the **Miramar Golf Club**, one that most people would agree is the best golf course in the city since it was reworked into a links-style course, pot bunkers and all, by former touring Australian professional, Graham Marsh, in the mid 1990s.

Miramar also sports an award-winning clubhouse to rival the new one at Waitikiri (see 'Christchurch Shores'). This one was designed by the Wellington firm of Warren & Mahoney.

The par-4 1st hole here is a medium-length par-4, but one of the most difficult opening holes in New Zealand golf even on a still day. The fairway bends around to the left to a split-level green with four bunkers in front and one in the back. Hit the ball left off the tee and you'll wind up in rough that is truly rough. Go right off the tee and you'll be lucky to avoid a stream.

The opening hole here sets the tone for the entire course. This one can rise up and bite you at any time, on any hole and more often than not when you least expect it. There are, after all, a total of 105 pot bunkers and, again, the rough can be rough or am I beginning to sound like a dog?

The front nine is about 600 metres longer than the back nine, but as veteran Radio New Zealand broadcaster and golfer extraordinaire, Garry Ahern, a member here, told me: 'You can play the front nine well and think you've got the course beat, only to lose it completely on the back nine.'

The 12th hole at Miramar is one of the best par-4s in the country, a true risk-and-reward hole that invites big hitters to go for the green in one, at the risk of three bunkers on the right and four around the green. That the wind is often at your back makes this shot more seductive.

A new drainage system, together with the course's sandy soil, means that even after the worst of the capital's winter rains, the course is still playable. GF: $45 AFF, $60 NON.

Karori Golf Club
Web www.karorigolf.co.nz
Phone 04 476 7337
Email karori@golf.co.nz

Mornington Golf Club
Phone 04 389 6816
Email mornington@golf.co.nz

Miramar Golf Club
Web www.miramarlinks.co.nz
Phone 04 801 7649
Email miramar@golf.co.nz

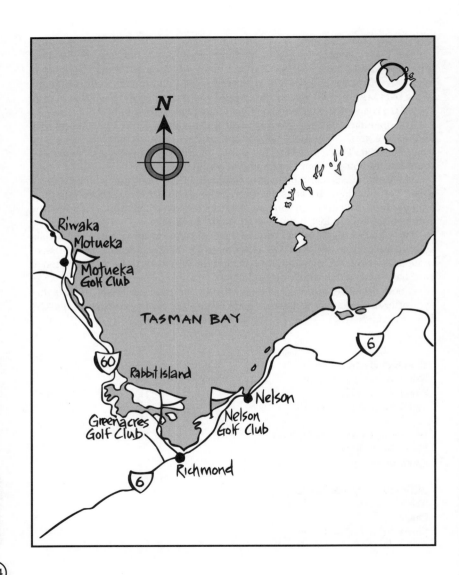

Tasman Bay

Nelson is named after Admiral Lord Nelson and, as many mad-keen golfers will surely want to know, it's the home of the only wearable art museum in the world. After all, golf may be the only sport known for its wearable art. There was Doug Sanders, who was as famous for the colour of his clothes as he was for that short putt that cost him the British Open title.

If you fly in, you'll see the **Nelson Golf Club** first from the sky, because it shares a fenceline with the Nelson airport. Once you're on the course the planes come in so low you might get the fright of your life if someone doesn't warn you first. Depending on the direction of the wind, one flight path is directly above the 11th fairway. It's a unique hazard, believe me.

The course also borders Tasman Bay, which makes it scenic but doesn't come into play — with one exception: the par-3 6th hole, which is 142 metres long for men; 132 metres for women. It's the club's signature hole and it's one of the best par-3s in the South Island. It plays right along the waterfront and if you go right at all off the tee, your ball goes out with the tide. The kidney-shaped green on this hole comes with pot bunkers in front and on the left. Under certain conditions this hole is a lot more difficult than its Number 17 Stroke rating suggests.

The par-4 14th also plays along the bay. However, a ridge (an old sand dune) acts like a levee and separates the fairway enough from the water that even the worst-case slice will not get wet. The obstacle here is not water: it's the extreme undulations in a fairway so fractured there may not be a flat square metre on it. To say this course is rugged is an understatement.

Although the club is the second oldest in the South Island after the Otago Golf Club (see 'Otago Nuggets'), it isn't clinging so much to tradition that positive changes aren't being made. The club is in the process of laying down luxurious couch grass fairways on all holes, a development that is sure to make Nelson a site for national and international tournaments. Kiwi touring professional

Richard Best holds the course record of 66. GF: $30 AFF, $40 NON.

Nelson has a host of motels to choose from, but you can get a 10 per cent reduction off your green fees at the Nelson Golf Club if you choose to stay at the Airport Greens Motel next to the course. The Boat Shed Café on Wakefield Quay is popular for its seafood; try the Beach Café for a hearty breakfast. If it rains and you're not into wearable art, take a tour of Mac's Brewery, one of the best boutique brewers in the country.

The next morning follow State Highway 60 around Tasman Bay to Motueka. It's a unique seaside drive. At the second roundabout before town, swing right and as you head towards the bay you'll see the sign for the **Motueka Golf Club**, sometimes referred to as 'Quay Links'.

Because the course is laid out over a sandy, gravelly soil (as you'd expect at a links) it drains so well that the winter months here might be the best time to visit. Only then are the nearby Western Ranges covered in snow.

The club has recently installed new irrigation that keeps the course looking fine all year round. Motueka has only 14 bunkers, two immediately in front of a severely sloping green at what might be the signature hole: the par-3 4th. In fact, the green slopes from back to front in a way that makes pin placement here critical. At the back it's no worries, too close to the front and a good shot might roll back into a bunker. Colin Williams, the greenkeeper here for more than 30 years, has never been known to be mean with his pin placements.

Some members will tell you that the best hole on the course is the par-4 6th — a dogleg right over a small rise to another sloping green with a bunker on the right. My personal favourite was the par-5 10th. It has a ditch and Out of Bounds down the entire right-hand side of the fairway, a new green (one of a series the club is installing), and a new pond, the only water hazard on the course. From the next tee players gain a sweeping view of the Tasman Bay across to Nelson and out to D'Urville Island.

If you choose to remain overnight in Motueka, try the Equestrian Lodge Motel, although with overnight accommodation in mind, club member Ken Osbourne is mad-keen to stage a tournament among players who, to qualify, must turn up in a campervan.

Score a hole-in-one here at the par-3 17th in any club-sponsored tournament and you'll win $1000 worth of clothing from a local shop. GF: $20 AFF, $25 NON.

If you drive back to Nelson after your round at Motueka, consider checking in at the Greenacres Motel for the night as it's right next door to the **Greenacres**

Golf Club, where you'll be playing on Day Three. The motel and the golf course are located about five minutes from the intersection of State Highway 6 and Queen Street in Richmond — the only traffic lights in Richmond.

Greenacres is a links that plays along the shore of Tasman Bay. However, it has a slightly different feel from the others because it's located on Bests Island, an island formed by the bay and the Waimea Estuary.

The terrain here is similar to what you've experienced at the Nelson Golf Club, where the fairways could pass for moguls were it a ski field. Only here there is an abundance of sandflies that act like flying obstacles. Tip: Bring sandfly repellent with you on this trip. But don't let those little buggers put you off, because the front nine here plays out across a small peninsula that's bordered on each side by water and feels so quiet and remote, if it weren't a golf course it might pass for a Buddhist retreat.

Here, the fairways aren't tight but the greens are small. Bunkers and the general windswept nature of the place make this course, 5600 metres long from the white tees, 5400 metres long from the yellow tees, more difficult than its length would suggest.

My favourite hole here was the 500-metre (white tees) par-5 7th called 'Long John'. It plays along the estuary and over a lumpy landscape to a small green with a bunker front right and water at the back that acts as a backdrop only. Harmless water, love it every time. GF: $25 AFF, $30 NON.

Nelson Golf Club
Web www.nelson.nzgolf.net
Phone 03 548 5028
Email nelson@golf.co.nz

Motueka Golf Club
Phone 03 528 8998
Email motueka@golf.co.nz

Greenacres Golf Club
Web www.greenacresgolfclub.co.nz
Phone 03 544 8420
Email greenacres@nzgolfcourses.co.nz

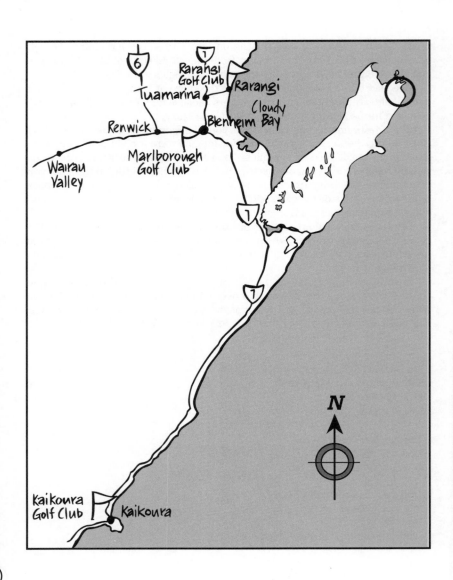

Marlborough Country

As anyone who drinks wine knows, the pioneers of viticulture who planted sauvignon blanc here in the late 1970s and early 1980s changed the nature of Marlborough forever. The worldwide demand for Marlborough sauvignon blanc is still greater than the supply. On the back of sauvignon blanc, Marlborough is producing world-class wines from other grape varieties too. So this is the perfect trip for mad-keen golfers who are also mad-keen about wine.

The Marlborough Hotel on Nelson Street (State Highway 6) in Blenheim is among the best choices for accommodation in town. Once you've checked in and sorted yourself out, head out again on State Highway 1 north toward Picton until you reach Tuamarina. Turn right and follow the signs to the **Rarangi Golf Club** on the opposite side of Rarangi Road from the sea, in this case Cloudy Bay.

This links is irrigated in places and the club was looking to install couch grass on some fairways. But that's an expensive proposition for a small club, so it may take a while. For the time being, visitors will have to contend with pea gravel.

Pea gravel is a coastal by-product of mainly small stones that's impossible to play golf on. It appears as barren stony patches about the course so for now, as way of compensation, players get a free drop should their ball come to rest there. The upside is this rocky soil drains so fast it's difficult for Hamish Parker, the club's new greenkeeper, to grow grass at all, hence the idea of laying down couch grass. Yet that's the character of this idiosyncratic course that looks and plays in every other way as a seaside links, one with some of the biggest and best greens in Marlborough.

Rarangi has 12 bunkers but it's not sand and gravel so much as the uneven lay of the land and the prevailing wind that make this course a test of the short and the long game. The course is 5900 metres long from the white tees; 5300 metres long from the yellow tees.

The signature hole here is the par-3 12th, with its infamous (as far as some members are concerned) long-grass hollow in front of an elevated, kidney-shaped green. This hollow would normally be a bunker but it's been left in long grass. Come up short of the green and it's possible to lose your ball!

A tee shot that clears the hollow with too much gusto risks running off the shoulders of the green at the back or along the side. The green is only 113 metres from the white and yellow tees, but even on the finest of days it will drive one or two players around the bend. GF: $15 AFF, $20 NON.

Back in Blenheim try Bacchus or the Hotel d'Urville for dinner.

The next day, leave early and take to the road again, to the **Kaikoura Golf Club** down the coast on State Highway 1. It's a scenic trip that takes about 90 minutes. Some golf clubs around the country, though established for many years, are now considering property development as a way of earning much-needed revenue for the club in order to continually upgrade the course. Kaikoura is one of them. The course is located about five minutes south of town on State Highway 1.

The club is sacrificing three holes on the back nine for a development that will mean creating three new holes elsewhere on the property. Though the town is a popular destination for whale watching, dolphin encounters, and swimming with seals, the golf course has no link, pardon the expression, to the sea. Indeed, the Seaward Kaikoura mountain range gives this course more of an alpine than seaside feel. Play here in winter and take a day off to ski on Mt Lyford.

This parklands-style course has only a small stream that only someone who has never swung a golf club might have to worry about and bunkers on three holes only. It's the small table-top greens that can be difficult to hit.

If you make this trip in October, who knows, you might be invited to play in the popular Lobster Inn Tavern Pro Am. Should you decide to spend the night, check out the options first on-line at www.kaikoura.co.nz. GF: $20 AFF, $25 NON.

Conclude your long weekend back in Blenheim at the **Marlborough Golf Club**, the oldest in the region, off State Highway 6 in Fairhall. The course is on Paynters Road, across from vineyards belonging to Villa Maria and next door to a new upscale housing community called Marlborough Ridge Resort.

The par-5 1st hole is 421 metres long for men and women alike but it's a dogleg right on such a narrow fairway that an iron, not a wood, is probably the better choice off the tee. The par-4 2nd is also 'target' golf. At 318 metres off the white tees for both men and women (no 'ladies tees' here) it's a decent length and a driver is the club of choice off the tee. However, the trick here is to keep your tee shot left and clear the side of a hill to a position on the fairway you can't see, or go right over the fence and wind up out on the road OB.

The 293-metre par-4 4th hole is only one of two holes on the course with water — a pond that most players should clear with their tee shot although, like the 12th hole at Takapuna, somehow this pond in front of the tee box can be a magnet for urethane.

For a peek at the new 'designer' homes popping up at the estate development next door you can drive around the corner to its formal entrance or stand on the tee at the par-3 5th hole. As you do so, you may also want to know that it was here where club regular Shirley Startup won a lovely garden swing seat when she knocked in a hole-in-one during the annual (and very popular) Alan Scott Wines-sponsored tournament that runs over three days in April. It was her *second* hole-in-one at that hole. GF: $20 AFF, $30 NON.

Rarangi Golf Club
Phone 03 570 5709
Email rarangi@golf.co.nz

Kaikoura Golf Club
Web www.kaikouragolf.co.nz
Phone 03 319 5628
Email info@kaikouragolf.co.nz

Marlborough Golf Club
Phone 03 578 7646
Email marlborough@golf.co.nz

Marlborough Country

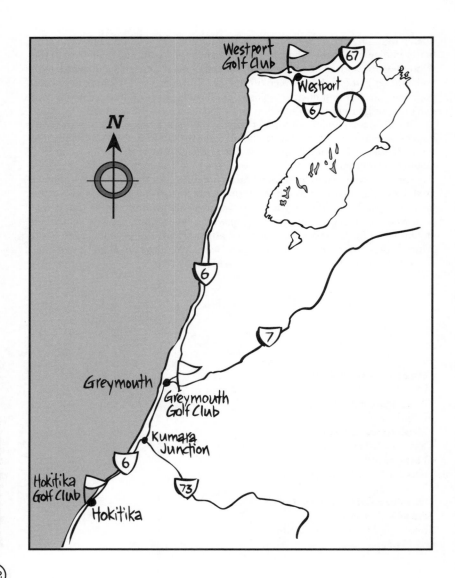

the Long Drive

Mad-keen golfers from the mainland already know this, so for the sake of readers from the North Island . . . it must be said first up that the three courses on this trip make for one of the best trips in this book, even if it means making a special effort to get there.

The West Coast is one of the country's most spectacular coastal drives, home to the majestic Southern Alps, the Franz Josef and Fox glaciers, the fascinating Punakaiki Rocks and beautiful pounamu, not to mention the annual Wild Foods Festival. But we'll leave deep-fried grubs and bush walks for another time.

The **Westport Golf Club** is south of town, across the Buller River (there's a new bridge!) at Carters Beach. It's a long drive from Christchurch or down from Nelson (allow five hours for both), but if you fly in you'll see the course because it's right next door to the airport, or rather the airstrip.

Westport, like Waipu on the east coast in Northland (see 'Northland Links'), was once a classic links overrun with pine. Although the trees offered some resistance to coastal winds, the downside was that volunteers were always out cleaning the course off after the too-frequent wind that left the place in a mess.

Like Waipu, Westport has cleared most of the pine away now so while it's more open and exposed, it's also a links that in places could truly be mistaken for one of those special relics from the Old World. Walk around here after dark and it wouldn't surprise me if you bumped into the ghost of Old Tom Morris.

Westport is where one pine tree grew too big for its own good. After too many members drove their ball into it too many times, they appealed to the committee to have it removed. When the committee refused, vigilantes took the matter into their own hands and, in the dead of night, cut the thing down themselves.

The fairways here turn dry and bouncy in summer but the greens are kept in excellent condition all year round. The par-4 4th hole is only 290 metres long and the par-4 10th is only 287 metres long, but because their fairways rise and fall and twist and turn in a way typical of the entire course, even big hitters with a lot of roll off the tee are not likely to reach those greens in one. Here there's really no such thing as a straight shot. You may hit the ball straight, but it rarely ends up that way.

The green at the par-3 2nd hole slopes steadily from back to front in the direction of a sand trap. Balls coming up short on the green commonly roll back into the bunker. It can be one of the toughest holes to par if the pin is placed in the front. As club captain Mark Millings said, 'We just hope our green-keeper hasn't had a bad night.' The club celebrated its 100th anniversary in 2005. GF: $20 AFF, $25 NON.

After your round at Westport, head down the coast 50 kilometres to Punakaiki, famous for its rock formations and blowholes. Spend the night at the new Punakaiki Rocks Hotel and Villas. The next morning drive on to Greymouth and to the richly green and pastoral **Greymouth Golf Club** located across the Grey River, about five minutes from town on State Highway 7.

In contrast to Westport, the course at Greymouth is a soft, lush parklands-style course whose character is determined more by the Grey River than the sea. The river is quite a way from the course but members still recall the flood of 1988, when the water reached the clubhouse walls.

Yet it's because the course plays over low land that it looks so deliciously green all year round. The fairways here are soft, so there's little or no extra roll of the ball. What you hit is what you get.

Only weeks before I stopped by, Sir Bob Charles himself had played here. He appeared as a special playing guest at a club charity fundraiser and while he was here he suggested (according to my sources) that the par-4 8th hole might be among the best 18 holes in the country. It's 329 metres long for men, 264 metres long for women; not so long, but the dogleg left is so acute you might think the leg was broken. It plays sharply to the left with OB on the left and, surprise, surprise, trees shutting off the fairway on the right. The hole didn't have a name that I could tell so for now I christen it 'Stephen King'.

The par-4 18th hole demands a perfect tee shot *and* a perfect approach through a narrow gap between the pine trees to a table-top green with a shoulder falling away on all sides. Inside the clubhouse are photos from 1980, when Sir Bob Charles, John Lister, Simon Owen, the Australian Rodger Davis and the Englishman Maurice Bembridge played an exhibition match here. Further along the wall you'll spot the Dagleish Shield, presented each year to the winner of the West Coast Interclub Championship. GF: $20 for all.

Complete your long weekend in Hokitika, the greenstone capital of New Zealand. The **Hokitika Golf Club** is just across the Hokitika River, two minutes from town — not that time is especially important here.

The course is wide open and windswept like a classic Scottish links and like an Old World links, it tends to play out and back along the shore. It's separated from the sea by an imposing line of flax and hearty bush, so there are no sea views. But by now, after driving down the coast from Westport, you'll have seen enough of the sea to keep you happy for a while. If you must, there's a short walk through the flax at the 10th tee.

Here, Mt Cook can be seen from the tee at the par-4 2nd hole on a clear day. The par-4 14th is known as Thompson's Corner, named in honour of Arnold James Thompson, one of the founding members of the club. Arnold was the father of current perennial club champion, Mike Thompson, and the grandfather of the club's most successful professional, Stuart Thompson, winner of the Tahitian Open, now a golf instructor at the Grange Golf Club in Auckland.

Mike Thompson and Barbara Nightingale have won the men's and women's senior club championship, respectively, more than 20 times. Stuart holds the course record of 61. Club member Lorna Clarke, 79 years old and still playing each week (and walking!) told me many mad-keen golfers from out of town stop here to play on their way to Franz Josef and Fox glaciers another 90 minutes or so further south. GF: $20 for all.

Visit the greenstone and precious-stone shops in town before you leave. The information centre in the middle of town carries a list of the available accommodation.

Westport Golf Club
Phone 03 789 8132
Email westport@golf.co.nz

Greymouth Golf Club
Phone 03 768 5332
Email greymouth@golf.co.nz

Hokitika Golf Club
Phone 03 755 8549
Email hokitika@golf.co.nz

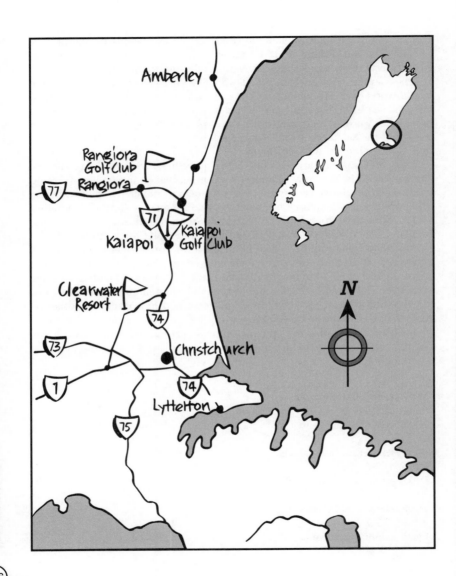

Christchurch North

If it's true that New Zealand has more golf courses per capita than any country in the world, then Christchurch may have more than any other city in the world, certainly the most of any city or town in New Zealand. A golfing trip to the 'Garden City' can therefore be planned in many different ways.

This trip begins north of the city in Rangiora, at the **Rangiora Golf Club**. The course is located off Kippenberger Avenue, on Golf Links Road.

The course at Rangiora dates back to 1908. It is now the home course of top Kiwi amateur, Ross Murray, who learned to play golf in Invercargill. It's a relatively flat, tree-lined course and trees pose the single greatest obstacle to a good score. The course is 6000 metres long for men, 5200 metres long for women. It's not short, and it also has six fairways that play around a dogleg left or right. However, the fairways are wide and the greens are kept in excellent condition, so with some luck a good score here is not beyond the reach of even a high handicapper.

The par-4 1st hole is only 312 metres for men, and 307 for women, but it plays along a tight fenceline (and the road) on the right that's OB. If you're not loose before you tee off here it's easy enough to slice your first shot of the day out of bounds. Overcompensate for the fence by hitting the ball too far left and you may still be on the fairway, but trees at the front left of the green make a clear approach from that side difficult.

The par-4 8th hole here, the Number 2 Stroke hole, is called 'The Pit' because a big dip in the fairway in front of the green often leaves players who come up short feeling, well, the pits. The green here is two-tiered, so knowing where the pin placement is on the day will make a difference to the club you use for your approach shot.

Rangiora is fair and fun. The 13th hole is 152 metres long for men, 145 metres for women. It ought to improve everyone's statistic for Greens In Regulation, as it might just possibly be the biggest green in the entire universe.

GF: $15 AFF, $20 NON.

Back down the road toward Christchurch, the **Kaiapoi Golf Club** recommends overnight accommodation at the Fairway View Lodge, a motel so close to the course it's possible to go between the two in a golf cart. But if you can, avoid using a cart when you play here because Kaiapoi, 'the Jewel of North Canterbury', is a beautiful course to walk. It is immaculately maintained with the help of a new computerised irrigation system that keeps it green and garden-like all year round. When the club calls it 'a jewel' they are not exaggerating.

The opening hole here may be the signature hole. It's a par-3 that, like the 1st hole at Rangiora, can give you more trouble than you need so early in the day. It's 159 metres long for men, 152 metres for women and its sloping green looks impossible to miss. But because it's the first hole of the day and you've rolled up, got out of the car, and rushed to the tee without stretching and getting loose (like most casual players) odds are you will miss it. In which case your ball will either end up too far left or right in rough or in one of the neatly trimmed green-side bunkers — and just like that your round begins with a bogey or worse.

This fabulous course is where Michael Campbell debuted as a professional and where Kerry Williams, one of Canterbury's top amateurs, still makes her stand. GF: $20 for all (a steal!).

Now that you're truly loose from two rounds in two days, you are ready for **Clearwater Resort**, one of the finest golf courses in New Zealand. Any mad-keen golfer will have seen it on television as it's the site of the New Zealand PGA Championship, a tournament that doubles as a US PGA Nationwide Tour stop as well. The resort is located on State Highway 1, five minutes north of Christchurch airport.

Clearwater, a man-made links with big, greedy lakes and bunkers waiting to drive you wild at every turn, is also wide open and exposed to the elements like no other in Canterbury. Playing here can be a test of character.

Outrigger Hotels & Resorts of Hawaii has taken over the management of the hotel and restaurant, so the quality of post-round service and comfort will make up for the humiliation you felt on the course.

With the Southern Alps framing the western horizon, you tee off. The 1st hole is a 361-metre par-4 from the white tees, a long dogleg left around wasteland and trees that some pros will drive over during the PGA Championship. Tip: If you are not a pro practising up to 20 hours a week and making money playing this game, stick to the fairways or Clearwater will turn you into a snack.

The course was designed by John Darby and Sir Bob Charles. It's laid out around a series of man-made lakes and it's beautifully maintained with finely manicured fairways and greens framed by brown tussock and stone.

The course has especially long tee boxes, not for aesthetic reasons so much as to reduce wear and tear from an active local membership and a regular inflow of overseas guests. Clearwater is a busy place. Subsequently, the distances from tee to green can vary a bit from day to day so if it matters to you (and it should), know where the pins are positioned on each hole before you commit because the greens here are fast and treacherous. With every hole pin placement determines how you approach it.

We could sit up all night arguing over a signature hole here. On the front nine I note the par-3 9th, 164 metres from the white tees across a lake to a green that slopes steadily from back to front. If the pin is at the back you risk going too deep and watching your ball carom off the cart path. If the pin is in front, you risk going too short, in which case that new $10 ball sleeps with the fish.

The par-5 10th plays left around a lake, the par-3 11th plays over a lake and by then, if the prevailing wind is blowing, you're blowing your mind.

The par-5 14th hole at Clearwater is one of the best par-5s in the country. It's a double-dogleg over two water hazards (streams) to an elevated green with bunkers in front. In this way, Clearwater is 'target golf'. Golf shots must be positioned and not just hit long. Here 'grip-it-and-rip-it' can work, but it's not always the most sensible approach. GF: $75 AFF, $125 NON.

Cushla McGillivray

See **Local Heroes**, *page 220*

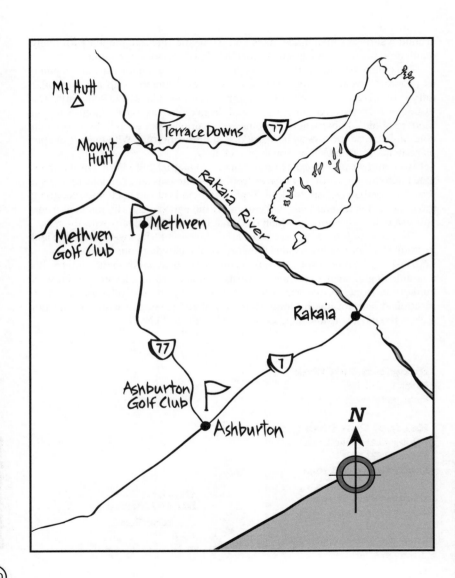

Mountains & Plains

The drive from Christchurch to Ashburton down State Highway 1 takes about an hour, although before you reach the town centre, you'll see the turn-off on your right onto Golf Links Road and the **Ashburton Golf Club**. Established in 1895, it's one of the oldest golf clubs in the country.

What else would a golf course in Mid Canterbury be if it were not dead flat? This quiet country track has fairways so wide even high handicappers can keep the ball in play — most of the time. Still, bunkers are a rare sight and the trees that shape the fairways are spaced enough to be relatively benign.

The course, 5800 metres long for men, 5100 metres for women, has not a single water hazard either, so if there's a noteworthy point of frustration to report it's the combination on some holes of grassy knolls near and around long narrow greens. Personally, I'd rather lie in a bunker than in long rough on the wrong side of a knoll.

The par-5 2nd hole plays to the left and then back right again to the kind of green noted above, only this one has a bunker at the back too. At the risk of winding up in sand (or 'on the beach' as my mad-keen brother likes to say) figure an extra club length if the pin is at the back.

On the back nine, the par-4 15th hole is average in length but the fairway turns left and into one of the longest greens on the course (45 metres). It's one of those greens where simply reaching it in regulation is no guarantee of a routine two-putt for par. Tip: Before playing this course practise your stroke for long putts. GF: $15 AFF, $25 NON.

After golf, check into the Ashburton Motor Lodge on the edge of town. The next morning drive north on State Highway 77 to Methven, that quiet little farm town that in winter turns into a busy hub servicing the skiing on Mt Hutt. Turn left onto Hobbs Road and you'll find the **Methven Golf Club**.

Before seeing it for myself, I had been told more than once what a great country course this was, and this proved to be true. On the day of my visit (midweek in February) no one was there except two young mothers happy to be playing golf again now that the kids were back in school.

This course is easy to walk, but it's hardly flat. The par-4 1st hole, for example, plays over a gully to an elevated green and the par-4 2nd hole is a slight dogleg left over a gully to a raised green with bunkers on each side. And so it goes, over an irregular landscape that marks the transition from the Canterbury Plains to the Southern Alps.

On the back nine, the par-4 11th hole plays adjacent to a shelter belt of Lawsoniana that's tall and solid enough to act like an imposing wall down the entire left-hand side of the fairway. The hole itself is straightforward and wouldn't be noteworthy were it not for the fact that Mt Hutt looms directly in the background like a reminder of who's really the boss in these parts.

The next two holes, although two of the shortest, are two of the best on the course. The par-3 13th is only 119 metres long for men, 105 metres for women, but it has a bunker directly in front of the green and the green slopes off sharply on all sides. The par-4 14th hole is barely over 200 metres long for both men and women but it has the only water hazard, a small pond, on the left and, of course, the green is on the left behind the pond. GF: $15 AFF, $20 NON.

From Methven carry on along State Highway 77 across the Rakaia River and gorge for two nights at **Terrace Downs**, one of the country's newest and finest high-country resorts. Look for the sign pointing left once you've emerged from the gorge on the other side of the river.

Terrace Downs opened in 2000 so the fact that it's relatively new means building, both private and public, is still going on. The main lodge houses a fine restaurant and pro shop; your accommodation will be in one of the spacious two-bedroom villas further along, past the tennis courts. Each villa has a balcony and sweeping views of Mt Hutt and surrounding farmland. At the time of my visit, plans were underway for a new hunting and fishing lodge and a new spa.

The golf course was designed by David Cox of Christchurch, with assistance from the Canadian firm Sid Puddicombe & Associates. It plays in full view of Mt Hutt and along the edge of the Rakaia River gorge, a locale the designers have used with great effect on the back nine.

The front nine play away from the gorge and among a new residential community forming here. The best hole here is the par-5 7th that sweeps over a hill and down to the left. It calls for a 'blind' second shot and because there's a lake bordering the right-hand side of the fairway below, big hitters especially risk ending up in the drink. Tip: Invest in a course guide-book before teeing off here.

The back nine holes at Terrace Downs are among the most spectacular golf holes in New Zealand because they play close to the gorge. For some, the par-3 16th might turn out to be too close. It's only 130 metres long from the back tees and 92 metres long from the front tees, but if you are too short or just slightly right your ball disappears over the cliff and though it may come to rest among the rocks and bush below, searching for it is not advised. And just as you would not want an angler hooking you by mistake, please refrain from hitting golf balls 'just for fun' into the river below. GF: $50 AFF, $90 NON.

Ashburton Golf Club
Phone 03 308 6371
Email ashburton@golf.co.nz

Methven Golf Club
Phone 03 302 8438
Email methven@golf.co.nz

Terrace Downs
Web www.terracedowns.co.nz
Phone 0800 465 373
Email info@terracedowns.co.nz

Mountains & Plains

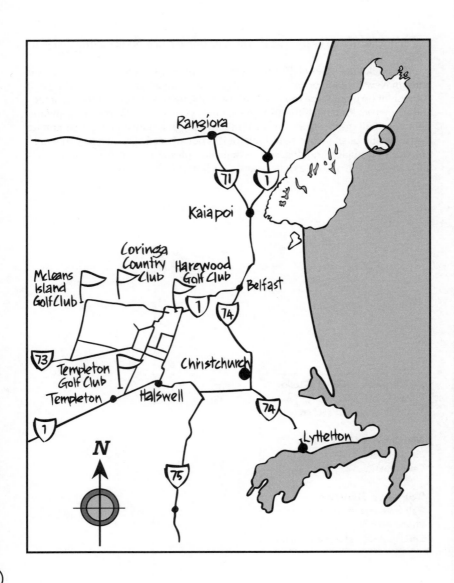

Christchurch West

Christchurch, the Garden City, is Golf City too. Just a few minutes south of the airport in Yaldhurst, on Pound Road, you'll find the **Templeton Golf Club**. Templeton is a country course that feels and plays like a links. Its extremely irregular terrain and gravelly soil is residue from the Waimakariri River as it has shifted course over time. In fact, the soil here drains so well the club has had to install a new irrigation system to prevent it from turning too brown in summer.

The fairways here are not tight, but they have their fair share of ridges, lumps and small gullies that are extremely irregular in a way that invariably leaves you confronting uneven lies, the ball resting either above or below your feet.

The signature might be the par-5 3rd hole, the Number 1 Stroke hole for men and women alike. It's less than 500 metres long from all three tees, but it has a small lake up the left-hand side of the fairway to a green with a bunker on the right. It's a classic risk-and-reward hole for big hitters. The rest of us lay-up and hope for the best.

The par-4 4th hole has a pond on the right not far from the tee. Still, a decent slice will wind up wet. Pull the ball too far left on this hole and you're certain to end up stuck behind a tree. Assuming you encounter none of this, your approach shot has to negotiate a kowhai tree directly in front of the green. Once while playing this hole even the quiet, understated Sir Bob Charles complained about this tree. Maybe he doesn't like yellow flowers. GF: $25 AFF, $35 NON.

The Airport Lodge Motel on Roydvale Avenue has advertised golf packages, but for the winter months only and for a minimum of four people. As you would expect, the options for accommodation in Christchurch are many and varied so check out www.christchurchnz.net to find something that works for you.

On the second day, drive north from the airport on State Highway 1 for two minutes to McLeans Island Road. Look for the sign to the Orana Wildlife Park, New Zealand's only open-range zoo with its compelling range of wildlife from all over the world. It's possible to hear lions roar from the first tee of the **McLeans Island Golf Club** across the road.

The McLeans Island course is 5700 metres long for men, 5300 metres for women. It's long, straight, and tree-lined tight but contrary to what the name might suggest, it has no water hazards. I never asked if Sir Bob had ever played here but my guess is he might not like the par-4 14th hole either.

This, the longest par-4 on the golf course and the Number 1 Stroke hole, is 350 metres from the white tees, and 334 metres long from the yellow tees. It's a slight dogleg with a cabbage tree right smack in the middle of the fairway about 150 metres from the green.

Cabbage trees are something of a feature here, for another one can get in your way at the par-5 18th. Local legend says: If the lions in the wildlife park across the road roar, rain is coming. GF: $25 weekends, $20 midweek for all.

The **Coringa Country Club** next door on the same road was the site of the 2006 New Zealand Amateur Championship. Arrive here as I did late on a Saturday afternoon and some of the members may be standing about with a cigarette in one hand and a pint in the other, a personal reward for completing another challenging round of golf. This imposing clubhouse was built in part with stones from the Waimakariri River.

Coringa is 6500 metres long from the back tees, making it one of the longest golf courses in the South Island. Uneven terrain, tight fairways, and sloping greens do not make it any easier.

On the front nine, the par-5 4th hole plays along the back boundary. It's a slight dogleg left with OB all the way on the left. Players must negotiate two gullies, one directly in front of a narrow green that's set slightly off to the left. Here, if your second shot does not come to rest on the right-hand side of the fairway, a large willow tree blocks any approach from the left. The par-5 6th hole is a double dogleg with a bunker directly in front of the green so even the best tee shot leaves you with plenty of work to do.

Out the back, the par-3 17th is 193 metres long and it plays to a green surrounded by three deep bunkers. Coringa has hosted national tournaments because it's a course that's kept in great condition all year round and it's not easy to score well here. Indeed, complete your round here and you too may feel in need of a smoke and a pint. The course record is 66, held by Aucklander Travis O'Connell, who set it at the 2006 New Zealand Stroke Play Championship. GF: $25 AFF, $30 NON.

McLeans Island Road could be called Golf Course Row because further along from Coringa is the **Harewood Golf Club**, one of only two clubs in New Zealand with two 18-hole courses. The other is Taupo (see 'Volcanoes & Lakes'). Here, if time is not on your side, play the Old Course. The New Course is shorter and friendlier for high handicappers and though it's a links-style course it's not as interesting in my view. The Old Course is more difficult but it's generally in better condition, and it has a history. The club was inactive during World War II because the Old Course, established in the 1930s, was a training ground for tanks.

As a testament to the quality of the Old Course, Harewood was chosen as the site for the 1997 New Zealand Men's Amateur Championship. In 1992, Michael Campbell finished runner-up here to Stephen Scahill in the South Island Amateur Championship.

The par-4 8th hole here is one of the best par-4s in the South Island. It's a long, sharp dogleg right that the truly big hitters will play by driving the ball over the top of pine trees at the corner. Still, to score par here approach shots must find their way through two big nasty pine trees and a bunker that form a passage to the green that's tighter than Cook Strait. GF: $30 AFF, $35 NON.

Templeton Golf Club
Phone 03 349 7571
Email templeton@golf.co.nz

McLeans Island Golf Club
Web www.mcleansislandgolf.co.nz
Phone 03 359 9768
Email mcleansislandgolf@paradise.net.nz

Coringa Country Club
Web www.coringa.nzgolf.net
Phone 03 359 7174
Email coringacc@paradise.net.nz

Harewood Golf Club
Web www.harewoodgolf.co.nz
Phone 03 359 8853
Email play@harewoodgolf.co.nz

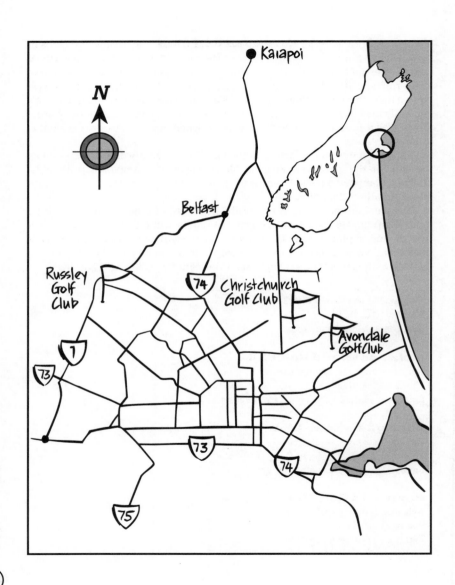

Canterbury Traditions

For me to provide readers with directions from Cathedral Square in Christchurch to the **Avondale Golf Club** would be like getting your directions from 'Wrong Way' Corrigan, the pilot who flew to New York only to end up in California. Christchurch, the Garden City, is lovely to look at but easy to get lost in. I had a map and still got lost.

Generally speaking, if you follow the Avon River and head toward New Brighton you'll find the Avondale golf course. Hey, I only had to ask for directions three times. Eventually, I reached the corner of Wainoni and Breezes Roads and voilà!

Avondale is an inner-city golf course (read: narrow, tight) known for its small, quick greens. It's only 5400 metres long for men, 5100 metres long for women because its position in the middle of an established Christchurch suburb has always kept it short and tight. Surrounded by suburbia as it is, it's possible to lose a ball OB on seven holes and of course if you by chance whack someone out walking the dog you're in more trouble still.

Avondale, founded in 1919 and the second-oldest course on this trip, is located in an area of Christchurch that's relatively flat and exposed to winds coming from all directions. The course is located on Breezes Road, after all, and the sea is only minutes away.

When I asked veteran Canterbury sports writer Bob Schumacher, a member here, for his favourite hole, he said the par-3 4th. It's 150 metres long and, as Bob noted, it's 'usually played with a crosswind coming off the sea. The green falls away to the right and the pin is often behind a sand trap on the right'.

In short, trust your swing but don't trust it too much.

Avondale has a series of short par-5s that will undoubtedly leave some hacks thinking they are ready to turn pro. That's why this is a good course to play first up on this trip because you'll need all the confidence you can get for the next two.

The par-3 18th hole here is 177 metres long for men, 142 metres for women and it's as deceptive as it is long. With a fence and OB all down the right to a deep gully next to a mid-sized green and a bunker opposite, it's easy for even the best players to come up short, or overcompensate and do as someone did on the day of my visit: blast the ball over the green into a clubhouse wall. GF: $20 AFF, $25 NON.

The **Christchurch Golf Club** is not far away. Simply follow New Brighton Road into Lake Terrace Road and you can't miss it — literally so, because the road winds through the golf course.

This is one of the finest golf courses in the land. Founded in 1873, 'Shirley' as the course is commonly called for the district of the city it's in, is the second-oldest golf club in New Zealand after the Otago Golf Club.

It was here on this site in 1910 that H. B. Lusk won the New Zealand Amateur Championship and ever since this most distinguished club has played host to a string of New Zealand Amateur and New Zealand Open championships, including the esteemed Eisenhower Trophy in 1990 and the New Zealand Women's Amateur Championship in 2005.

The opening hole here is a sharp dogleg right that plays inside one bunker and over another, around a eucalyptus grove, to a kidney-shaped green, so shaped because the 1st and 17th pins are at different ends of the same green.

The 1st hole was once deemed too dated, too easy perhaps for modern equipment, so Australian legend Peter Thomson, winner of five British Opens, was called in to re-work this hole and others on the course.

He installed a number of new bunkers about the course that are visually quite stunning — when you finally see them. Some, like the ones at the par-4 6th hole (across the road from the clubhouse), cannot be easily seen from the tee. Local knowledge is an advantage here.

The bunkers here are fantastic to look at, not so hot to play from. Some are like sink holes, out of sight and out of mind, until you're in them; others rise up menacingly, in clear view.

The 12th hole here is a 410-metre (white tees) par-5 but titanium drivers, a new generation of long-flight balls, and the desire of the club to continue its tradition of hosting top tournaments, has forced the club to transform it into one of the toughest par-4s in the country. A (hidden) bunker in the middle of the fairway calls for a tee shot slightly left or right. The hole plays upslope and around a slight dogleg right to an elevated two-tiered green.

After a teenage career learning to play the game at Masterton, Sir Bob

Charles was a member here. It was from here that he launched his remarkable career and for that reason he remains the club patron today.

Drive back out toward the airport on Day Three to the **Russley Golf Club** on Memorial Avenue. You'll know you've arrived when you pull in next to a red-brick building that at first appears more like a fortress than a golf clubhouse. It was completed in 1994 and was so much the talk of the town that the Sultan of Brunei, on a visit to Christchurch, had to see it for himself.

Russley was established at its current site in 1927, after moving from a 12-hole course at Hagley Park. This course has hosted a number of men's and women's national championships and it's well known as the site of the Garden City Classic, a popular professional tournament played here in the 1970s.

The course is kept in immaculate condition, and the fairways and greens are among the best in the South Island. It's 5700 metres long from the white tees, 5400 metres long from the yellow. Typically, a long par-4, in this case the 9th hole, is the Number 1 Stroke hole. But if there is a signature it might be the par-5 6th that plays away from the clubhouse to a corner. It has a small lake to the left of a two-tiered, narrow green.

The club motto is 'Medio Tutissimus Ibis'. I asked Ernie Poole, a member and rule interpreter here, what that meant and he replied: 'Hit the bloody ball down the middle!' GF: $40 AFF, $60 NON.

Avondale Golf Club
Web www.avondalegolf.co.nz
Phone 03 388 8203
Email avondaleoffice@paradise.net.nz

Christchurch Golf Club
Web www.christchurchgolf.co.nz
Phone 03 385 9506
Email enquiry@christchurchgolf.co.nz

Russley Golf Club
Web www.russleygolfclub.co.nz
Phone 03 358 4748
Email proshop@russleygc.co.nz

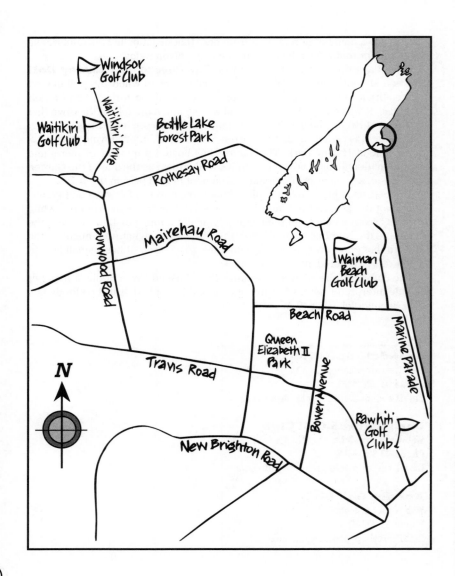

Christchurch Shores

At New Brighton Beach, on Marine Parade just north of the pier, you'll find the **Rawhiti Golf Club**. It's located in the same domain as other local sports clubs; in fact, if you're coming into the centre of town on New Brighton Road, turn left where the AA sign reads Archery Club.

Rawhiti has 12 sand traps, but then it's a links course so it doesn't need too many. It's by the sea so maybe that's why it has no water hazards, either. The only devil of a thing visitors have to concern themselves with here, apart from the usual pine trees, is an OB pathway that splits the course in two.

Rawhiti is owned by the Christchurch City Council and as a municipal golf course it's of a comparable standard, for better or worse, to Wellington's Berhampore only this course, though not entirely flat, is not played out over steep hills (see 'Wellington City'). There it's generally up-and-down, here it's up-and-back.

Rawhiti is a good place to begin this trip because it's inexpensive and it's not especially difficult. It also serves to acclimatise visitors to playing by the sea if they've just flown in from, say, Alice Springs.

Rawhiti professional, Lynne Shaskey, is one of the rare female head professionals in the country. GF: $14 midweek, $17 weekends for all.

Further north, less than five minutes away by car and equally close to the seashore, is the **Waimairi Beach Golf Club**. It's tucked away between an old subdivision and a new one off Bower Avenue. QE II Park is nearby. This is where current New Zealand touring professional, Tony Christie, learned to play the game.

This is a links but the combination of fairways and greens kept in good nick and tall pine trees acting like shelter belts leaves this course looking and playing more like a parklands-style golf course.

Known locally for its quick greens, the par-4 1st hole, 366 metres long from the white tees, plays straight between two veritable walls of pine that define the first fairway and act as shelter from offshore winds. The green has a narrow gateway between a bunker on the left and a hill on the right.

When an easterly sets in, the 329-metre (white) par-4 5th transforms itself from the Number 8 Stroke hole on the course to the Number 1, for it plays directly into the wind. In that way Waimairi is by the sea, but apart from the tee box at the 12th hole, sea views are blocked by a new housing development next door. Of course, they do help to lessen the wind that on some days can turn this normally docile seaside links into the Creature From the Black Lagoon. GF: $25 AFF, $30 NON.

From Waimairi Beach, drive north on Burwood Road past the hospital and you'll come upon Prestons Road and the **Waitikiri Golf Club**, one of the finest courses in Canterbury with a new clubhouse straight out of the pages of *Architectural Digest*. It seems the old weatherboard clubhouse, however elegant it might have been, was costing too much to maintain. The club replaced it with a post-modern mix of steel, glass, and canvas (the sail look) in a way that at first seems incongruous with a lovely, refined golf course established in the 1930s. Still, the facilities are new and the view of the golf course from the restaurant is perfect. You can have lunch and watch others three-putt the 18th green.

One of the best holes on the course is the 177-metre (white) par-3 3rd that for most of us calls for a long-iron or fairway wood off the tee. The trick is to avoid OB on the right and such a steep drop-off on the left that some players have been known to go left and never return . . . just kidding. There's a big fat green-side bunker, of course, and the green slopes severely from back to front.

The par-5 4th was re-designed to increase its degree of difficulty. It appears straight on the scorecard but it's actually a dogleg right with a bunker at the elbow (just where you don't need it) and water left of the green. The par-4 18th, by the way, bends right around a giant poplar tree that makes this one of the best finishing holes in Canterbury — even if you do three-putt in front of 50 people having lunch. GF: $30 AFF, $50 NON.

The **Windsor Golf Club** right next door to Waitikiri is so close a stranger might stand on the first tee of one thinking he's playing the other. Windsor is 5400 metres long from the blue tees, 5050 from the yellow tees. It plays around the former Bottle Lake, now so overgrown it's a bird sanctuary.

The short par-3 16th hole here is a little gem. From a lofty tee box men and women players alike require only a short-iron to reach the green below. The only catch: a sand trap directly in front of the green. Thus, the tendency is to be too short or too long or so intimidated by this little beast that you shank the ball into the bush. I was there only a few minutes and I saw that happen twice.

The par-5 10th swings around the swamp, or rather, the lake . . . in a way that leaves those who slice or even fade the ball too much playing a new ball. Tip: At the 10th and 18th greens try to avoid hitting the innocent pukekos with your approach shot. Someone did that once and the club had the bird stuffed and set in a glass case and called it a trophy — one that's now held by either Windsor or the Harewood Golf Club as the prize for winning their annual dual-club competition. The Pukeko Classic? GF: $10 AFF, $15 NON.

Rawhiti Golf Club
Phone 03 388 7408

Waimairi Beach Golf Club
Phone 03 383 0408
Email waimairi.beach@golf.co.nz

Waitikiri Golf Club
Web www.waitikirigolf.co.nz
Phone 03 383 1400
Email admin@waitikirigolf.co.nz

Windsor Golf Club
Web www.windsor.orcon.net.nz
Phone 03 383 1403
Email windsor@golf.co.nz

Christchurch Shores

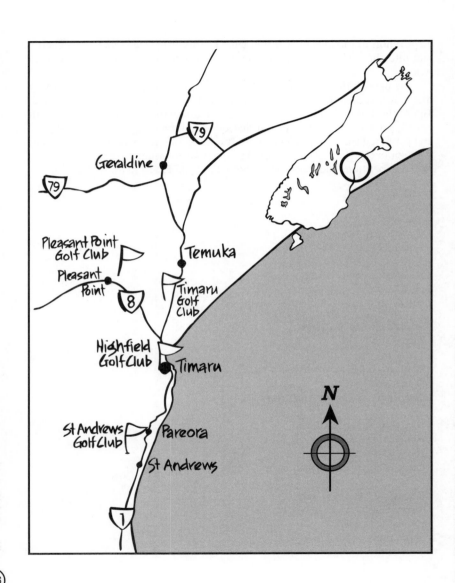

45

Aorangi

You can drive to Timaru or, I note, Air New Zealand flies in four times a day from Wellington. All the major rental car companies have an agency there, even Rent-A-Dent. But before you get too far, **Timaru Golf Club** is next door to the airport, so why not make that your first stop on this tour.

If there is a single name associated with Timaru golf it's John Lister. Lister grew up here. All three golf courses on this trip can claim a piece of him but at this course, more commonly known as 'Levels', Lister still holds the course record: 64. It's been equalled once, in 1973 by club member Graham Brown.

Inside the clubhouse is a photo of Lister holding high the trophy after winning the 1970 New Zealand PGA played at Mt Maunganui. In that tournament the young man from Timaru who awed spectators with his monster drives shot four rounds of 65-66-65-66.

A 64 here, meanwhile, is an especially good score because the course is long (6050 metres from the blue tees), over fairways that tend to be wide enough to keep even high handicappers happy, but are broken up by grass mounds and gullies, dips and sudden turns. Still, it may not be the long game that counts most here as the short game.

The knolls, white-sand bunkers, and uneven greens combine in ways that can turn monster drives into wimpy ones. Take the par-4 7th hole for example. It's a long dogleg left with trees (of course) and a bunker lurking at the turn. If off the tee you successfully get through the corner (Lister would drive *over* the corner), your second shot is to a green that slopes front-to-back and left. Meanwhile, the par-4 18th takes no prisoners. It sweeps around left over a gully to a green with big bunkers on each side and a steady back-to-front slope.

George Morrison, a member who I happened to meet in the pro shop, told me he thought the best time to play here was in winter, on one of the clear, crisp days when the Southern Alps are covered in snow. GF: $25 AFF, $35 NON.

Check into the Panorama Motor Lodge overlooking Caroline Bay. If it is a cool winter's night, spend a few minutes in the sauna or the spa before dinner at any one of the fine cafés below on The Terrace.

The **Highfield Golf Club** is on Douglas Street in Timaru. Highfield was the original site of the Timaru club before it moved out to the airport. Council had control of this course for a while then leased it to the current club. The club hired a real greenkeeper and the course is now in the best condition it's ever been in and improving all the time. The course is laid out over a big slope at the back of town, so it tends to play either up a hill or down one, with some exceptions. The par-4 7th hole is called 'The Ridge' because that's what it is up the back and it's from there players can gain a view of the town and the bay.

This course plays up-and-down but it's not long or difficult, just a lot of fun. And once you're through the front nine it flattens out. The 13th and 14th holes are back-to-back par-3s while the long par-4 18th (367 metres from the blue tees) is one of the best closing holes in South Canterbury. It bends left to a green squeezed tightly between Douglas Street (OB) and the clubhouse. The fairways can be rough in spots but the greens are in good condition. GF: $15 for all.

The **St Andrews Golf Club**, 12 kilometres south of Timaru on State Highway 1, has claimed to be the only 'St Andrews' golf club outside Scotland. However, the Hamilton Golf Club is also called 'St Andrews' so maybe the difference lies in an official name versus an unofficial one.

In any case, this St Andrews is a gem. The course is located across the main highway from the ocean. It has features of both a links and a parklands-style golf course and it has both mountain and sea views.

Here the fairways are wide but treacherously uneven, a quality highlighted by a deep and sometimes hidden creek that snakes through the course. The picturesque opening hole is a mild-mannered par-4 dogleg left that's framed on the right by a neatly trimmed shelter belt. It's not a long hole so a fairway wood off the tee is sufficient to reach the turn, perfect for travellers who have not fully stretched before they play.

The par-4 4th hole can play with the wind at your back and because it's only 269 metres long from the blue tees, it's tempting on those days for even a mild-mannered hack to go for the green in one. But few realize that dream here because even the best tee shot invariably gets hung up in one of two gullies cutting across the fairway directly in front of the green.

The name of the course is *not* derived from its famous Scottish namesake. It's named for the district where it's located; one named after Andrew Turnbull, the first manager of the New Zealand Australia Land Company. He was given the nickname 'Saint Andrew' because he swore a lot. GF: $15 AFF, $20 NON.

Take a short drive along State Highway 8 from Richard Pearse Airport in Timaru to Pleasant Point. Here, it must be said, more visitors probably come to experience steam locomotion than play golf. Pleasant Point has two fully operational steam trains and the world's only remaining Model T Ford railcar. They run daily during the summer over two kilometres of track built by volunteers, some of them perhaps the same people who expanded the **Pleasant Point Golf Club** from nine to 18 holes not so long ago.

The golf club plays along the main road into town, but the car park is back down Butlers Road a kilometre or so before the town centre. The original nine holes seen from the main road are part of the Pleasant Point Domain, where golf is played alongside rugby, soccer, tennis, netball, and frisbee golf.

Only three holes on the front nine (the original course) dogleg one way or the other; the rest are straight and flat, with no water hazards or sand traps to get you, uh, steamed up. In the early 1990s, the club decided to expand the course to 18 holes so the back nine was built entirely by volunteer labour. Here they created a course in view of the Southern Alps with more dips and turns and nuances than the original nine. GF: $15 for all.

Timaru Golf Club
Web www.timaru.nzgolf.net
Phone 03 688 2405
Email timaru@golf.co.nz

Highfield Golf Club
Phone 03 688 8413
Email highfieldgc@xtra.co.nz

St Andrews Golf Club
Phone 03 612 6590
Email standrewsgolf@xtra.co.nz

Pleasant Point Golf Club
Phone 03 614 7304

John Lister
See **Local Heroes,**
page 221

Aorangi

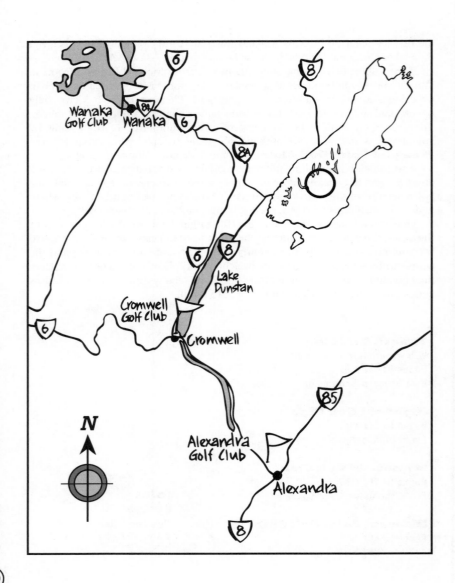

Central Otago

The drive on State Highway 6 from Queenstown, New Zealand's tourism capital, into the heart and pinot noir soul of Central Otago, is one that everyone on the planet should do before they die. It's a short drive that winds through the Kawarau River gorge, which is as naturally beautiful as it is dramatic. In fact, if it's not dramatic enough try A J Hackett's bungy jump. It's just on the left as you enter the Gibbston Valley. Chard Farm winery will be on the right.

If you can hold your taste-buds at bay for half a day, leave the turn-off to the wineries at Bannockburn (Felton Road and Mt Difficulty, to name two) for later in the day. For the moment (and because I say so) you are going straight to the Cromwell town centre, where it's impossible to get lost. Be careful not to run over tourists taking photos of the giant fruit. The pear, the apple, and the peach (or is it a nectarine?) are artificial but what the heck, they're *big*.

The **Cromwell Golf Club** is located behind the Golden Gate Lodge and the Lake Dunstan Motel, the latter offering special stay-and-play packages at certain times of the year. The golf course, also known as 'The Dunes', looks, feels, and plays like a classic links even if the nearest body of water of any size is Lake Dunstan across the road.

The course is played over sandy soil but the many lumps and bumps in the fairways are shaped by tailings dumped here in the gold-mining days. This is especially true on the last five holes, the original holes on the course. The other holes have been added since but they complement the original five very well. Tussock and marram grass add to Cromwell's Old World look.

Club general manager Doug Harradine thought the par-4 8th hole might be the signature hole and he could be right. It's 363 metres long off the white tee, a dogleg right on a tight, uneven fairway that tends to slope left to right. It's the Number 1 Stroke hole.

The par-4 11th hole is shorter and only the Number 16 Stroke hole, but it's called 'Sailor' after one of the greatest mad-keen golf dogs that ever lived.

Sailor was a legendary Cocker Spaniel who was sniffing around here one day and in no time found more than 200 lost golf balls! He became a club mascot and in time, as these stories go, a club hero. There was only one slight problem: Sailor was so mad-keen he brought back balls that weren't lost too. GF: $25 AFF, $35 NON.

Now you can taste wine in Bannockburn, five minutes away, and the Bannockburn Hotel, all done up, is a good choice for accommodation and meals too.

The next day follow State Highway 8 over to Alexandra, site of the annual Blossom Festival. Stop briefly at the lookout over the still-impressive-after-all-these-years Clyde Dam.

The **Alexandra Golf Club** is on State Highway 8 north of town. Buildings and other structures in Central Otago are unique for the use of stone, especially the schist that comes with the territory. So it's only appropriate that the 1st tee here is built up like a small stage and supported on all sides by walls of the flat stone. It's a perfect introduction to the territory.

The par-4 1st hole here is only 319 metres off the white tee, 292 metres off the yellow tee. But for men and women alike a drive too far right will more than likely wind up in one of three decent-sized bunkers that highlight the turn of this slight dogleg left, where the approach to the green is narrow enough as it is.

The par-3 6th hole plays down from an elevated tee to a mid-sized green with a small club-built water hazard on the right. But here the committee was kind, for it's a shallow pool that, if you like, you can take your shoes off and wade into to retrieve your ball. Or you can see just how waterproof those new golf shoes really are.

The water hazard at the par-4 18th hole is also committee-made but it's utterly unique because someone, a landscape architect perhaps, had the idea of placing a tree in the middle of it. It's a small but highly unique water hazard.

The greens are generally accompanied by at least one bunker, if not two, and often a grassy knoll or three. But for the most part they are flat and what you see is what you get. GF: $25 AFF, $35 NON.

If you didn't get enough wine-tasting at Bannockburn then you may wish to drive four kilometres from Alexandra out to Earnscleugh Road to Black Ridge, a winery that claims to be 'the southernmost winery in the world'. Try the Alexandra Avenue Motel or the Alexandra Motor Lodge Motel if you wish to stay overnight.

The trip over to Wanaka on Day Three is another compelling road trip, this one north on State Highway 6 up the shores of Lake Dunstan. Of course, it's the seductive combination of mountains and lake that make the **Wanaka Golf Club** one of the most get-out-the-camera golf courses in the country.

Located as it is on a hillside with the Southern Alps towering above and Lake Wanaka and the town below, it's not surprising that one in four permanent residents here belongs to the golf club. The course is only 5700 metres long from the back tees but who needs long when you've got terrific views from the green of the very first hole? The opening hole here, like so many others on this course, is scenic. But it plays upslope and is a testy beginning to a golf course that for all the sightseeing can suddenly turn into a reality check.

Having a golf course in the foothills of the Southern Alps means land is precious. That goes some way towards explaining why the fairways at Wanaka are generally tight with little room for error — unless you like playing your second and third shots off the wrong fairway.

Players (and I use the term loosely) unable to hit a golf ball straight will find this course beautiful but deadly. Seven of the first nine holes have OB on the right and most of the holes on the back nine are OB on the left. For overnight in Wanaka try the Edgewater Resort Hotel. GF: $30 AFF, $50 NON.

Cromwell Golf Club
Web www.cromwellgolf.co.nz
Phone 03 445 0165
Email cromwell@golf.co.nz

Alexandra Golf Club
Web www.alexandra.nzgolf.net
Phone 03 448 8374
Email alexandragolf@xtra.co.nz

Wanaka Golf Club
Web www.wanakagolf.co.nz
Phone 03 443 7888
Email wanaka@golf.co.nz

Central Otago

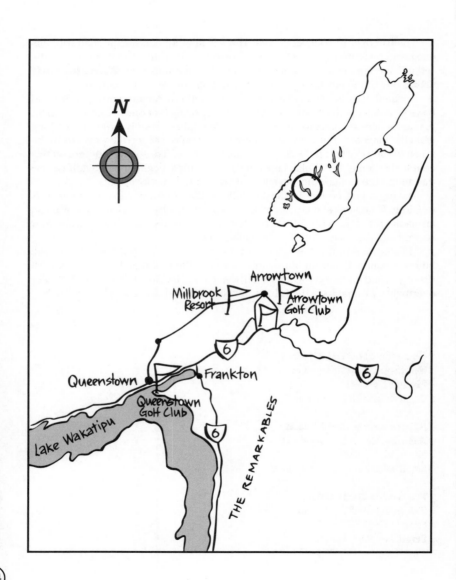

Queenstown

Queenstown is, of course, the hub of tourism in New Zealand and one of the world's most popular destinations for people who live for an adrenalin rush. Then again, there's always that gentle trip down Lake Wakatipu on the *Earnslaw*. Whatever, Queenstown is altogether such a busy fun-spot you may feel like a little peace and quiet for a change.

Go with golf clubs in the boot of the car out to Lake Hayes, where you'll turn left off State Highway 6 to the **Millbrook Resort**. Millbrook is a full-service alpine resort with upscale residential housing and accommodation, casual and fine-dining restaurants, an indoor fitness centre and heated pool, tennis courts, and a new spa.

The golf course, designed by Sir Bob Charles, has wide-open fairways that leave even the worst mis-hits off the tee in play. Trust me. Millbrook has a small lake and in places long grass and bush but it's still difficult to lose a ball here. It's a golf course players of all abilities can enjoy, especially when the sun is shining and the stunning mountain landscape all around is covered in snow. Even in winter, when most visitors are flocking to the skifields nearby, Millbrook can be played in light clothing.

The only way to lose a golf ball at Millbrook is to hit it in the water, which comes into play significantly on the par-5 5th hole and the par-5 18th hole. The tee at the 5th is worth a longer stop than usual because it's one of the highest elevations on the course. Push your tee shot too far right here, however, and you may see your ball plop out of sight in one of the two small lakes at the turn of a hole shaped like a big banana.

How big a banana you are might be decided at the par-5 18th hole. Here the green with a slope from back to front is directly across a pond. Big hitters have to make the big decision to go for the green in two and risk ending up in the water, or laying-up short and playing the hole more conventionally.

A course map will show still another pond at the back of the par-3 13th hole, but have no fear for this pond is too far back of the green to be a real threat. The 13th tee, however, is elevated a bit and another prime spot to scan this extraordinary mountain locale.

Former European Tour winner and popular Kiwi professional, Greg Turner, is working with the resort to develop another nine holes here. Golfers should take advantage of the resort's stay-and-play packages that include multiple nights' accommodation, breakfast, and golf. GF: $55 AFF, $70 NON for in-house guests all year. 1 October–31 March $70 AFF, $125 NON. 1 June–30 September $55 AFF, $85 NON.

Arrowtown, another regular stop on the tourism trail, is just over the hill from Millbrook. The **Arrowtown Golf Club** is through town, past the quaint set of shops, and out the back on Arrow Junction Road toward State Highway 6.

This golf course is loaded with character, thanks mainly to the schist outcrops and a severe ridge-and-valley terrain. Arrowtown is only 5400 metres long for men, 4970 for women, but it can be fierce. Take the par-4 8th hole, for example. It's only 288 metres long for men and women alike. But rocky outcrops favour no one and on this hole players have to play around (or over) five such outcrops with their approach shot.

The par-4 18th hole here is only 324 metres long for men, 275 metres long for women. But it plays down a narrow chute to a dogleg right with a pond on the left. Use a driver off the tee at your peril. If you lay-up short of the water with a fairway wood or a long-iron off the tee, you still have to clear a deep gully with your second shot to reach an elevated green that drops off sharply on the left.

Where being long off the tee at Millbrook can be an advantage, Arrowtown is more 'target golf', where position on the fairway, not length off the tee, matters more. The greens here are relatively small. The one at the par-3 16th hole is the narrowest green in the world *and* it has large mounds and bunkers on each side. Arrowtown is like a terrific links-style course only it's surrounded by mountains — if you can imagine that. GF: $25 AFF, $40 NON.

On Day Three head back into Queenstown, but rather than follow the main road into town, turn left at the airport. Further along, you round a bend and come upon the right turn to Kelvin Heights and the **Queenstown Golf Club** at the tip of the Frankton peninsula.

This highly scenic golf course features one of the most photographed holes in New Zealand golf: the par-4 5th that plays around the edge of Lake Wakatipu to an elevated, two-tiered green. Photos of this hole commonly feature the snow-capped Remarkables in the background.

The scorecards list this hole as the Number 1 Stroke hole on the course and maybe it is when the prevailing wind is kicking up white-caps on the lake. But the par-4 11th hole is no 'cake walk' either, for it plays upslope and over a ridge with a 'blind' second shot that must be kept left for a clear third shot into a green set back off to the right.

The other especially photogenic hole is the short par-3 10th that plays from an elevated tee down to a green with the lake and Walter Peak in the background. A small Douglas fir tree stands directly in the flight path of a tee shot from the white and yellow tees, though not from the blue tee. But for all, the green drops off the back so steeply that it appears to drop off into the lake.

This lovely golf course was built by the members themselves in the 1970s. As with the other courses on this trip, snow rarely accumulates on the fairways here so that even in winter it's possible to combine skiing with golf. In November the club hosts the Skyline Classic, a popular social tournament followed by dinner up the gondola at the Skyline Restaurant. GF: $30 AFF, $50 NON.

Millbrook Resort
Web www.millbrook.co.nz
Phone 0800 800 605
Email reservations@millbrook.co.nz

Arrowtown Golf Club
Web www.arrowtowngolf.co.nz
Phone 03 442 1719
Email info@arrowtowngolf.co.nz

Queenstown Golf Club
Web www.queenstowngolf.co.nz
Phone 03 442 9169
Email info@queenstowngolf.co.nz

Greg Turner
See **Local Heroes**, page 221

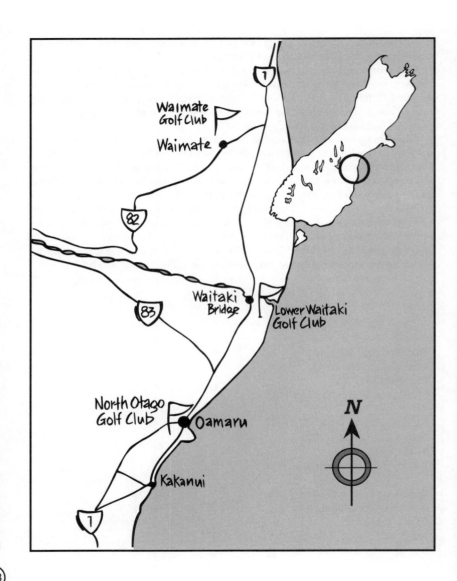

North Otago

Oamaru has an airport, but on the day of my visit it was closed. However, if you're wanting to get there by plane, take note that Oamaru is little more than an hour's drive from the Timaru airport or less than two hours from Dunedin.

Oamaru was the original home of New Zealand writer Janet Frame. Literary references from her novel *Owls Do Cry* are now the basis of a 'Janet Frame Trail' and anyone familiar with the work of the New Zealand Historic Places Trust will know that Oamaru has the finest singular collection of Victorian buildings in the country — all made of limestone from the local quarry. A penguin colony and the **North Otago Golf Club** are not far away, though my guess is the penguins don't play golf.

Tip: When playing golf in Oamaru, try to avoid playing in a southerly. A southerly can turn the North Otago golf course to a bitter chill even at the height of summer. The course is located south of town and it plays over hills and gets great sea views in places, although if you see white-caps you'll probably need a warm jacket. Even in the middle of summer.

Gaining sea views, however, means towing a trundler up the hills. North Otago hires carts, but if you are truly mad-keen then walking is part of the adventure of playing here.

Take the par-4 3rd hole, for example. Assuming your tee shot winds up on the flat, your second shot is to a green up the hill. It's a small hike. But the 3rd hole leads easily enough to the 4th that plays along the top and the 5th, called 'Seaview', will reward you for your effort. So what if you're six strokes over par already?

After playing one of the longest and tightest holes on the course, the par-5 12th, players use a footbridge to cross *above* Kakanui Beach Road. Four of the 18 holes here are played on that side of the road. Cross back over again to play (downhill) the par-3 17th.

The par-4 18th hole here is a solid finishing hole. It's average in length but it plays along the road with OB on the right and, as if that was not enough, the fairway slopes severely from left to right. I was left wondering how many times someone has stood on the 18th tee here with a good round behind them only to score double or triple bogey on this last hole. Bugger.

If that happens and you lose it completely, chill out by driving further along the road to the spectacular Kakanui Beach. Because State Highway 1 is further inland, Kakanui is one of the few places along this coast that feels wild and remote. Back in town, we spent the night at the Bella Vista Motel and ate and drank ourselves silly at Fat Sally's.

Drive north from town the next day for about 10 minutes, past the (still closed) airport, to the **Lower Waitaki Golf Club**. Watch for the sign and the turn-off to the right over the railway tracks. After walking a hilly golf course the day before, Lower Waitaki will feel like a reprieve. It's as flat and as player-friendly as they come. Lower Waitaki is not far from the sea, so scoring well here will depend on the conditions.

Yet this is an easy-going parklands-style course, not a links course. The fairways are wide and the greens are generous. What few bunkers there are on the course are relatively benign. There is a small pond to the left of the 9th green, another near the 18th green, and a third to the left of the 15th green. But water comes into play only when it rains.

The clubhouse is built in part from the same limestone that makes this region unique. This may be the only golf course in New Zealand where you place campervan fees and green fees through the same slot. GF: $15 for all.

The quiet country town of Waimate, the birthplace of Norman Kirk and the site of an annual buskers festival, is a short drive further north off State Highway 1. You'll find the **Waimate Golf Club**, the prettiest of all on this trip, out the back of town off Parsonage Road. Stop in town on your way for a coffee at the Wildberry Café. The visitor information centre, where you'll find options for accommodation, is not far away.

Small-town courses like Waimate can have a full-time greenkeeper but little money is left over for more detailed upkeep. They rely heavily on member-volunteers. Often these courses, though out of the way, can be among the best-kept because the volunteers look after them like their own garden.

In that way Waimate, though it plays over the foothills of the Hunter Hills, is a garden-like experience. The native trees planted here are especially noteworthy and the layout of the course itself is unorthodox. The 9th and 10th greens, usually close to the clubhouse, are away here.

The course is divided by Browns Road, with nine holes on one side and nine on the other, albeit not the front nine and back nine as such. The par-3 7th hole plays over a gully to a plateau-like green with bunkers on both sides. The club's brochure describes this as the easiest hole on the course but really, is there ever an 'easy' hole on a golf course?

The par-4 5th hole plays next to Browns Road. It's a dogleg right up the hill to a 'blind' green and it has a dam and OB on the right. The par-4 14th hole and the tee box at the long par-4 18th will give you a good view of the territory. GF: $15 for all. Norm Kirk is buried in the cemetery along McNamaras Road.

North Otago Golf Club
Web www.northotago.nzgolf.net
Phone 03 434 6169
Email north.otago@golf.co.nz

Lower Waitaki Golf Club
Web www.lowerwaitaki.nzgolf.net
Phone 03 431 3800
Email lower.waitaki@golf.co.nz

Waimate Golf Club
Web www.waimategolf.co.nz
Phone 03 689 7009
Email admin@waimategolf.co.nz

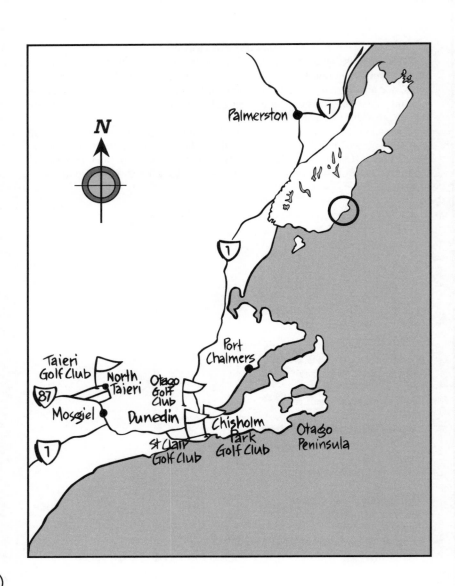

Otago Nuggets

Dunedin hosts a summer festival each year that includes events like the **Robbie Burns Birthday Party**, a performance by the **Piping and Dancing Association of New Zealand** and an **Octagon Plaza Art Exhibition**. Summer is the best time to visit, of course, because it gets chilly here in winter.

Mad-keen golfers here have grown to accept playing in high winds and even rain. As John Humphries, the greenkeeper for more than 35 years at the **Chisholm Park Golf Club** told me, 'Unless it's blowing, it's not golf!'

Chisholm Park is a 'hidden gem' of a golf course. The course is located south of the harbour on the coast. The 10th tee overlooks Tomahawk and Smails beaches to the north, St Kilda and St Clair beaches to the south. It's magnificent.

The course played host to the men's New Zealand Amateur Championship in 2003 and while many of the young guns who now turn out for this tournament could drive the par-4 3rd hole, for it's only 259 metres long, many walked off with a bogey or worse. Why? Because this hourglass-shaped green is elevated and uneven, and so small that big hitters can drive the distance but often can't hit the green. Steep shoulders on three sides, long grass at the back, and pot bunkers all around make this hole akin to a minefield.

The series of four holes, from the par-5 8th to the par-5 11th, are the most spectacular because they play along the cliff. The 8th hole plays up a steady slope and around a dogleg left to a green that first appears to be teetering on the edge. Your second shot on this hole is 'blind'. You won't see the green, so either walk to the top of the ridge and have a look or ask someone who knows where to aim — or risk hitting your ball into the Southern Ocean. The par-4 9th hole plays along one cliff, the par-3 10th along another. GF: $20 AFF, $30 NON.

The **St Clair Golf Club** is high on the hill at the south end of St Clair Beach. You can see the top of its pine trees from Chisholm Park, but unlike Chisholm Park, St Clair is so high above the coast that it plays more like a parklands-style course than a links. This course has stunning views of its own and a rich history too. In the 1970s St Clair was the site of one of the best professional golf tournaments in the Southern Hemisphere, the Otago Charity Classic. Take time while you're here to peek inside the clubhouse and you'll see photos of the legendary Sam Snead, who played here in 1976. The great Spaniard, Seve Ballesteros, won the tournament in 1977, and Aussie Ted Ball set the course record of 63 when he won the New Zealand Open in 1979. Kiwi Simon Owen was runner-up that year.

The 2nd tee here has terrific views of Dunedin Harbour, but it's the tee at the par-4 15th hole that most visitors come away talking about. It's situated in the far corner of the course, on the edge of the cliff with a coastal view that rivals, say, the views of the coast at Kauri Cliffs. A signpost here points the way to the South Pole, 4913 kilometres away.

The hole is a straight, relatively easy par-4, only like most holes on this course the green is anything but flat. The par-4 18th hole here plays over two gullies and a rollercoaster fairway to a green that's so close to the clubhouse that if you go too long with your approach shot, you'll break a window of the Ladies Lounge. GF: $25 AFF, $35 NON.

If you want to get into the country for a day, drive down the southern motorway to Mosgiel and follow the signs from there to North Taieri, about five minutes away. There, on Milners Road, you'll find the very fine **Taieri Golf Club**. The opening hole here is a short par-5, but a stream cuts across the fairway short of the green making this a true risk-and-reward hole. Big hitters can reach the green in two on a perfect day, the rest of us carry on as usual. Tip: The green on this hole is elevated so the second shot plays longer than it looks. A charming stone bridge over the water adds to the scenic quality of this hole.

The par-4 6th hole here is a signature hole. It's only 264 metres long from the white tees, 250 metres long from the yellow tees, so many players, men and women alike, will use a fairway wood or even a long-iron off the tee.

But it plays out to a *three-tiered* fairway (the only one in the country?) that sweeps to the right over a pond to a small, compact green flanked by bunkers. The par-3 7th plays back over the same water. GF: $20 AFF, $30 NON.

No long weekend golf trip to Dunedin would be complete without a round at the **Otago Golf Club**, commonly known as 'Balmacewen', the oldest golf course in New Zealand. Founded in 1871, the club has a wealth of history. Over the years many of the top players in the world have played here, including Arnold Palmer in 1966. Balmacewen is where J. McGregor won the first club championship in 1872. It's where J.N. Lemon, now a life member, scored 10 holes-in-one over his 53 years playing here, and it's where the likes of New Zealand touring pros Greg Turner and Mahal Pearce developed their skills.

A display case inside the clubhouse is like a potted history of golf. It features clubs and balls from the early 1800s including a club used by the Scot Tom Morris, whose father Old Tom Morris was one of the founders of the game.

A noteworthy hole here? All of them. Yet the short game matters more here than the long drive. The par-4 8th, for example, is only 270 metres long from the white tees, so why did I score a double bogey? I missed the green to the right off a steep shoulder and . . . you don't want to know the rest.

Arnold Palmer birdied the par-4 11th when he played here. Famously known as 'The Glenn', it's one of the longest drops from tee to green in New Zealand. Reaching the green here in two is not such a big deal (Palmer drove it in one) but because the green rolls toward the centre and out again, two-putting for par is not easy. The club has installed a unique rope tow to help older players up a steep path to the 12th tee. GF: $30 AFF, $60 NON.

Chisholm Park Golf Club
Web www.chisholmlinks.co.nz
Phone 03 455 0565
Email pro@chisholmlinks.co.nz

St Clair Golf Club
Web www.stclairgolf.co.nz
Phone 03 487 7076
Email st.clair@golf.co.nz

Taieri Golf Club
Web www.nzgolf.org/taieri
Phone 03 489 7450
Email taieri@golf.co.nz

Otago Golf Club
Web www.otagogolfclub.co.nz
Phone 03 467 2099
Email info@otagogolfclub.co.nz

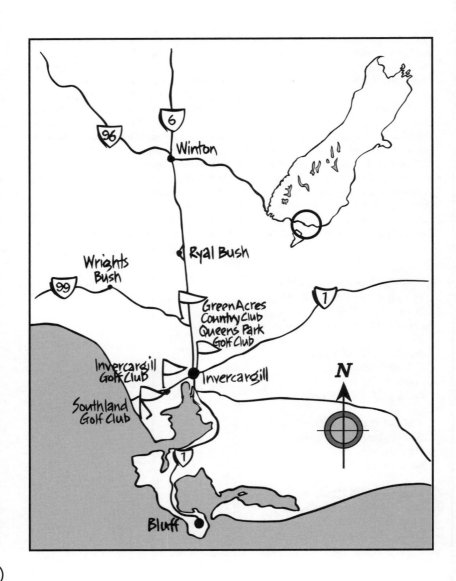

Deep South

Invercargill was originally planned as a 'one-mile square' by a surveyor named J.T. Thomson. Thomson later became New Zealand's first Surveyor General, an appointment that came about in no small way because of what he did here, setting out a town in a street grid around a series of reserves — a re-creation of Victorian England if you wish.

That legacy can still be seen today, only now one of those reserves is a nicely maintained golf course. You'll find the **Queens Park Golf Club** on Kelvin Street. It's the largest and most centrally located reserve Mr Thomson left behind, so you can't miss it. Queens Park is as user-friendly as a town course can be. It's a flat, straightforward, tree-lined course with big fairways and dance-floor greens with few if any tricks.

Trees are obstacles here as they are anywhere else, of course, like at the par-4 opening hole. In this case, a grove of oversized pines tower over the fairway at the elbow of a dogleg left, narrowing the gap there enough to force you to think about club selection from the start. Taking the driver out of the bag first thing here may not be a good idea — unless you're over 50 years old.

Generally this council-owned track, with no water hazards or fairway bunkers, is nicely cut and clear-cut in a way that makes for a good start to this southernmost golf trip in the world. GF: $10 AFF, $15 NON.

Drive out of town about eight kilometres toward Winton on State Highway 6 the next morning to the **Green Acres Country Club**, the longest course in Southland. The course plays about 5900 metres from the white tees, about 5000 metres from the yellow tees.

I asked a couple of old boys sitting in the sun with a coffee and a smoke why the 1st hole was called 'Embarassment'. 'Because everyone is watching you tee off,' was the reply. The 1st tee here is right by the clubhouse and the only driving range in Invercargill. The hole is a straight par-4 over a rolling fairway that's especially tight down the left, enough to force many tee shots too far right into trees. Go left or lose your ball in the trees at the right off this tee and you may hear someone behind you making a distinctively Southland wisecrack.

The course is long, but being long isn't always the best approach. The par-4 5th hole, for example, is a sharp dogleg right but it's short and here again, using a fairway wood or a long-iron off the tee will be best for some players. The par-4 13th hole here is one of the sharpest doglegs in the country, as it cuts back left at a perpendicular angle.

A small pond comes into play on the par-5 10th hole, but you can't see it from the lower end of the fairway. First-time guests ought to be clear about where the water is before they play a second shot on this hole. All the fairways are finely cut and a deep, solid rough more than compensates for the few sand traps. GF: $14 AFF, $25 NON.

The **Invercargill Golf Club**, or 'Otatara', is the most established club in Southland because it's been around since 1900. In that way it rivals the likes of the deeply traditional clubs elsewhere, such as the Christchurch Golf Club and the Royal Wellington Golf Club.

Here, in December 1934, Gene Sarazen, winner of the British and US Opens two years before, turned up for a game. In more recent times one of the country's current professional tour players, Steve Alker, set the course record of 64, one he shares with two others.

The course sits in a lowland and because Southland rarely suffers from drought, the fairways can be soggy after rain. But that also means the greens and fairways are in excellent condition all year round, even in summer when other courses can turn brown and hard. Playing at Otatara is like playing through a lush, green park, although one with drainage ditches coming into play.

The par-4 3rd hole, the Number 1 Stroke hole, is often described as a 'dogleg left' but it's not that so much as a fairway with a huge mound on the left-hand side. Players have the option of trying to play over it or around it. Tip: Do what they do in Rome and stay to the right.

The signature hole here is the par-3 17th that plays from an elevated tee down to a tight, elongated green with two big bad bunkers on the right and two more on the left. All the bunkers on this course, I noticed, were finely cut, a sure sign the club has a greenkeeper who cares. GF: $20 for all.

The **Southland Golf Club** is only five minutes further along the road from Otatara. Turn left at the Sandy Point recreational reserve, where outdoor pursuits stack up like a supermarket counter. The golf course is last on the block after rowing, archery, clay-pigeon shooting, and stock cars.

Oreti Sands takes so much pride (and rightly so) in being the southernmost 18-hole golf course in the world that the general manager Colin Conway happily presents a certificate to visitors saying so. It reads: 'Congratulations on playing the most southern 18-hole links course in the world.' You fill in your own name and if someone from the club doesn't sign it, sign it yourself.

Scrub and dunes shelter the course from the Foveaux Strait so it's only from selected elevated tees that players gain anything of a sea view. The first and one of the best is at the tee of the par-3 3rd hole. From here visitors can see Bluff Hill to the east and the snow-capped Takitimus to the west.

The par-5 2nd hole here is short but it has the biggest green in the Southern Hemisphere. The hole plays around a fence (OB) on the left and though a big hitter will drive over the fence easy enough and be in position to reach the green in two with an iron, once there the green slopes steeply from back to front in a way that makes pin placement on the day critical — saying nothing of what the wind might be doing. GF: $15 AFF, $20 NON.

If it rains, drive the Invercargill Heritage Trail. If you've never seen a kea, visit the Queens Park Aviary. Try the Ascot Park Hotel for reasonably priced accommodation and good food or go on-line to www.invercargill.org.nz. Try the Tuatara Café at the corner of Dee and Esk streets for good coffee.

Queens Park Golf Club
Web www.queenspark.nzgolf.net
Phone 03 218 8371
Email queens.park@golf.co.nz

Green Acres Country Club
Phone 03 215 9016
Email greenacrescountry@xtra.co.nz

Invercargill Golf Club
Phone 03 213 1133
Email igc@paradise.net.nz

Southland Golf Club
Phone 03 213 0208
Email oretisandsgolf@paradise.net.nz

Ross Murray
See **Local Heroes**, page 222

Local Heroes

Ted McDougall
Mangawhai

Born in Scotland, you might say Ted McDougall came to golf naturally. But after his father moved the family to New Zealand after the war, young Ted was as keen on soccer as golf. The family settled in Pukekohe, where Ted joined the golf club. Soccer was soon left behind when, with Sir Bob Charles, Stuart Jones, and John Durry, he became a member of the New Zealand team that played in the first-ever Eisenhower Trophy, established in 1958 by American President Dwight D. Eisenhower.

McDougall turned professional shortly after, but declaring yourself a professional golfer in the 1950s was like trying to win a lottery today; only geniuses and fools ever succeeded. McDougall had two children, so he gave up the gamble for the certainty of teaching. As an amateur again he found happiness *and* success.

He raised his family and won four inter-provincial titles for Waikato, and represented New Zealand nine times. Since 1986 he has been the manager of the Mangawhai Golf Club and is one of the most sought-after instructors in the country.

One day a stranger from Minnesota turned up to play Mangawhai, and as he was paying his green fees mentioned that he was a member of a certain golf club in St Paul. Of course he assumed McDougall would not have heard of it. Of course he had. By chance McDougall's uncle, Jock, was the professional there!

Frank Nobilo
Waitakere

Born and raised in the Auckland suburb of Sandringham, Nobilo has often been mistakenly related to the wine-making family of the same name. Today, he promotes Nobilo Wines but he's not directly related to the family. Nobilo played his golf in the early days out of the Waitakere Golf Club and in the late 1970s he was selected multiple times for New Zealand junior teams. In 1978 he won the New Zealand Amateur Championship, turning professional the following year at the age of 19.

His stellar pro career took a couple of years to develop, however, for it wasn't until 1982 that he won his first tournament, the New South Wales PGA. He remained a consistent winner worldwide after that. His victories included two New Zealand PGA titles and nine wins on the European PGA Tour. He also won the Mexican Open and in 1997, playing the tough US PGA Tour, he won the Greater Greensboro Chrysler Classic. He represented New Zealand 11 times in the Dunhill Cup and he was a three-time Presidents Cup selection. A chronic back injury forced his early retirement. He lives today in Florida where he is an analyst for The Golf Channel.

Marnie McGuire
Remuera

Introduced to golf by her father David, a scratch player and club champion at the Remuera Golf Club, McGuire also won her club championship more than once before she stunned the golf world in 1986 by becoming the youngest player to win the Senior British Amateur Championship.

In the late 1980s she was a scholarship player for four years at Oklahoma State University, where she was a first team All American selection. She returned home from the United States and after winning a series of domestic tournaments she headed off again, this time to Japan. There she played on the professional women's tour for seven years, winning five times. In 1999 she returned down under to win the Australian Open. She was later named New Zealand Sportswoman of the Year. She's now retired from the rigours of professional golf tours, lives in Auckland, and devotes her time to coaching young New Zealand prodigies.

David and Sheree Smail
Waikato

They met at the Hamilton Golf Club ('St Andrews') in 1985 and were married 10 years later. They now have two children and were New Zealand's only husband-and-wife touring professionals.

Sheree, originally from Matamata, began playing golf at the age of 15 and soon became a successful Waikato representative as an amateur. She turned professional in 1990 and joined the Australasian Ladies Tour before playing in Japan, where she won the Fuji Sankei Open in 1993.

David, born in Hamilton, began playing golf at the age of 12 and quickly grew into a top Waikato amateur who represented the province and New Zealand multiple times. He turned professional in 1992 and for four seasons played on the Australasian PGA Tour.

He won the New Zealand Open and the Canon Challenge in Australia in 2001, but began playing regularly in Japan, where he has won five times, including the Japan Open in 2002 and the Casio World Open twice. More recently he won the Bridgestone Open in 2005. Sheree, meanwhile, retired from playing in 1996 to start a family and manage her husband's career.

Janice Arnold
Waikato

Born in Morrinsville in 1962, Arnold was the first New Zealand woman to play on the professional Ladies European Tour. She turned pro in 1985 after a stellar amateur career representing Waikato and New Zealand multiple times. As an amateur she won the New Zealand Stroke Play Championship. She played on the European Tour for 15 years, winning once, at the St Moritz Classic played at the Engadine Golf Club in Switzerland. Her other best finishes include a third place in the 1991 Ford Ladies Classic and another third-place finish at the 1994 Dutch Open. She had 18 top ten finishes altogether and a career-low round of 63 before retiring in 1998. She lives in Surrey, England today where she teaches golf at the Rusper Golf Club.

Phil Tataurangi
Waitomo

He was just seven years old when he began caddying for his father at the Waitomo Golf Club. By the time he was 10, he'd been selected to attend a regional golf school held by Alex Mercer, who was coaching several top Australasian players — most notably Steve Elkington — at the time. The following year, at the ripe old age of 11, he won the senior men's club championship at the nine-hole Puahue Golf Club near Te Awamutu. He represented New Zealand internationally numerous times as a teenager and in 1992 he was a member of the New Zealand team (with Michael Campbell, Grant Moorhead and Stephen Scahill) that won the Eisenhower Trophy.

The following year he won the New Zealand Amateur Championship and shortly after that he turned professional. His first tournament as a pro was the US PGA Tour Qualifying School where he won his playing card and in 1994 was the youngest player on the tour. There he met and played with his boyhood hero, Jack Nicklaus, and in 2002 he won The Invensys Classic in Las Vegas. A debilitating back injury in 2003 required surgery and for two years Tataurangi's career was on hold. But like his pal Michael Campbell, he has made a courageous comeback and at the start of 2006 he was back playing on the US PGA Tour.

Bradley Iles
Mount Maunganui

There was a time in New Zealand when golf was perceived as a sport for older people only. Younger people played rugby and cricket and waited for the right moment to take their OE. Today, a combination of programmes initiated by the NZ Golf Association, good instruction from coaches like Mal Tongue, and the success of New Zealand professionals overseas, has produced a new generation of young guns, among them Bradley Iles.

Iles, born in 1983, began playing at the Mount Maunganui Golf Club. He represented the Bay of Plenty as an age-group player and then played for Wellington's senior team before being selected to play for New Zealand at the age of 18. His victories since include the Asia Pacific Junior Match Play

Championship, the South Island and North Island Amateur Championships, and the Australian Amateur Stroke Play title. In 2003 he shot a 63 in tournament play four times. His career nearly ended tragically, however, after a fall off a golf cart in the United States in July 2004. A serious head injury left him in a coma for three days but he recovered slowly, returned to New Zealand, and today he's back playing local and regional professional tournaments with the aim of returning to the States to play, someday, on the US PGA Tour.

Brenda Ormsby
Rotorua

Ormsby, one of the most talented players never to play on a professional tour full time, began playing golf at the Rotorua Golf Club's nine-hole course when she was 10 years old. By the age of 17 she had moved to Te Puke and, playing out of the old course there (no longer in existence), she became a New Zealand representative for the first time, playing in the Tasman Cup.

Representing the Bay of Plenty countless times, she has won the New Zealand Match Play Championship three times and the New Zealand Stroke Play event seven times, one year shooting 19 under par over four rounds to win the stroke play.

Her career spans three decades. In 1984 she was the leading individual scorer in the Queen Sirikit Cup and as recently as 2003 she won the New Zealand Stroke Play title for the seventh time. Today, she is the club professional at the Springfield Golf Club in Rotorua, where she lives.

Kapi Tareha
Napier

His father, Kurupo Tareha, was the paramount chief of the Ngati Kahungunu tribe and a patriarch of golf in Hawke's Bay. Indeed, Kurupo Tareha won the New Zealand Amateur Championship in 1903. But it is the son, Kapi Tareha, who became a legend as the first (unofficial) long-drive champion of New Zealand. Members of the Napier Golf Club, where he played and where his descendants retain special playing rights, still talk about the day Kapi teed off at the par-4 18th hole and drove the ball through the green and into the car

Local Heroes

215

park! This in the days when golf clubs were little more than wooden hammerheads attached to a hickory stick and golf balls were wound in cloth and rubber.

Tareha won oodles of trophies playing golf yet he was also one of the country's foremost all-round athletes, excelling in rugby, boxing, and athletics. He was the captain-commander of a New Zealand contingent that attended the coronation of King Edward VII following the death of Queen Victoria.

The foyer of the clubhouse at the Napier Golf Club is highlighted by a beautiful carving by Taka Walker that commemorates the golfing father-and-son legends. It includes the original club used when he struck his famous blow.

Stuart Jones
Hastings

The late, great sportswriter Sir Terry McLean believed that Stuart Jones was the second-greatest New Zealand golfer ever, after Sir Bob Charles. Sir Terry, Sir Bob . . . makes you wonder why S.G. Jones, commonly known as 'the Emperor', wound up with a mere MBE. Someone should write to Buckingham Palace and remind them that Jones won seven New Zealand Amateur Championships, a Canadian Amateur title, two professional tournaments as an amateur, and was a New Zealand representative on seven Eisenhower Trophy teams, including the very first with Sir Bob, Ted McDougall, and John Durry (who coined the nickname).

Jones represented Hawke's Bay 32 times. Among his most cherished memories are that inaugural Eisenhower played in Scotland at St Andrews where he met Bobby Jones, and 5 February, 1972 at his own beloved Hastings Golf Club, where he shot 30 going out and 30 coming in.

The Jones family owned and operated Bon Marche department stores in Hastings and Napier, and with his father and three brothers minding the store, 'The Emperor' could get away long enough to take part in amateur tournaments. His golf profile also lent success to the family business. However, he never turned professional — a lonely occupation — because he enjoyed the team spirit of amateur golf more. And, as he told me for this book, 'Golf is a wonderful game when it's going well, but when it's not, it drives you nuts.'

Jones, now in his eighties and still playing regularly at the Hastings Golf

Club, has 'shot his age' so many times he's stopped counting. He is a member of the New Zealand Golf Hall of Fame.

Craig Perks
Palmerston North

Perks grew up in Palmerston North, where he was born in 1967. He honed his skills at the Manawatu Golf Club playing with the likes of Grant Waite, with whom he eventually headed overseas, to the University of Oklahoma. But while Waite remained in Oklahoma, Perks transferred to the University of Southwestern Louisiana from where he launched his professional career in 1993.

The transition from amateur to pro status was not easy. He spent a number of years playing minor tours in the US and though he won four times on the Hooters Tours he repeatedly failed to earn his PGA Tour card. He attended qualifying school, or 'Q School', nine times before he made the big time. By then his name had almost been forgotten at home and no one following the US PGA Tour really knew who he was until he won the 2002 Players Championship in the most exciting finish in the history of that tournament. Playing the difficult TPC Sawgrass course in Florida, he chipped in for an eagle at the 16th hole, sank a long, difficult putt for a birdie at the 17th, and then chipped in again for a birdie at the 18th hole. Even veteran observers said it was the greatest finish to the so-called '5th Major' they had ever seen.

Grant Waite
Palmerston North

Growing up in Palmerston North, Waite was a New Zealand junior soccer rep before devoting most of his time to golf. Playing out of the Manawatu Golf Club, a club that spawned current US PGA Tour player Craig Perks and Waite's current fellow Nationwide Tour colleague, Tim Wilkinson, he must have known he was onto a good thing when he won the Australian Junior title.

He soon headed off to the University of Oklahoma, on a scholarship, where he was a three-time All American selection before he turned professional in 1987. He has since represented New Zealand five times at the Dunhill Cup. His biggest win came in 1993 on the US PGA Tour when he won the Kemper Open.

Local Heroes

Simon Owen
Wanganui

Owen was born in Wanganui, where he learned to play golf with his brothers Craig and Paul at the Castlecliff Golf Club. In 2005 he was named the club's patron. After a stellar amateur career representing Wanganui-Manawatu in two Freyberg Rosebowls and twice winning the Wanganui-Manawatu Stroke Play Championship, he turned professional in 1971.

As a pro, Owen promptly set about making his mark internationally by winning tournaments in Fiji, Germany, and Scotland. He returned home to win the New Zealand Open in 1976 and he represented New Zealand at three World Cups and two Dunhill Cups. In the 1980s he won the South Australian Open and three domestic pro tournaments in New Zealand, including the Hawke's Bay 72-Hole Classic (twice).

His most successful season was 1978 when he won the New Zealand PGA Championship, the Malaysian Dunlop Masters, and finished runner-up in the World Match Play Championship at Wentworth and the British Open at St Andrews, the latter won by Jack Nicklaus.

He closed the first phase of his pro career by winning tournaments in Tahiti and Fiji in 1991. Today, the second phase, he competes on the European PGA Seniors Tour where he has won in Tunisia and New Zealand. He lives at Kinloch, at the new Jack Nicklaus Signature golf course that's set to open in 2007.

Sir Bob Charles
Masterton

Born in Carterton in 1936, Charles established his early reputation as an extraordinary golfing talent at the Masterton Golf Club. He moved to Wellington where, as an 18-year-old bank clerk playing as an amateur, he won the New Zealand Open in 1954. Six years later he turned professional and in time became the greatest left-handed player in the world, highlighted by his 1963 British Open victory at Lytham St Annes.

After many years playing successfully on the US PGA Tour, Charles turned 50 in 1986 and joined the US Senior Tour (now the Champions Tour). Since then, he has won more than 20 senior tournaments worldwide, including the

Senior British Open at Lytham. In 2004 he retired from playing in the New Zealand Open, a tournament he had won three times. It had been 50 years since he first won that tournament and he remains the youngest player ever to win it. He is today the country's foremost senior ambassador for golf, the patron of the New Zealand Golf Foundation, and a member of the New Zealand Golf Hall of Fame. When he's not overseas he lives today in Canterbury, where his farm at Oxford is called, suitably enough, 'Lytham'.

Lynnette Brooky
Wellington

One of two New Zealanders playing on the Ladies European Tour, Brooky learned to play golf in Wellington, where she was born in 1968. She was one of a crop of talented youths coached by Mal Tongue at the Manor Park Golf Club. As an amateur she won the New Zealand Open twice and was runner-up at both the Australian and the British Stroke Play championships. She turned professional in 1994 and after four top ten finishes in Europe she recorded her first victory at the Austrian Open in 1998. She has since won the French Open twice.

In 2005 she represented New Zealand at the Women's World Cup of Golf. Back on tour she recorded seven top ten finishes including three third-place finishes at the Samsung Masters in Singapore, the Italian Open, and (her favourite tournament no doubt) the French Open. She is New Zealand's most accomplished female professional golfer, having played in 156 tournaments worldwide, twice shooting her all-time low round of 64.

Michael Campbell
Wellington

Michael Campbell became the second New Zealander after Sir Bob Charles to win a major golf title when he captured the US Open at Pinehurst, North Carolina in 2005. That year he also won the World Match Play Championship.

Campbell was born in Hawera but learned to play his golf on a scratchy nine-hole track at Titahi Bay, a course that doubled as a sheep paddock. He won the Australian Amateur title in 1992 but his local fame grew even more when he won the prestigious Eisenhower Trophy, a world amateur team event, with Phil Tatearangi, Grant Moorhead, and Stephen Scahill. He turned professional the following year and wasted no time in winning his debut tournament, the Cannon Challenge in Australia.

Two years later he became an international name when, after leading the British Open going into the final round, he finished third. His career was then suddenly in jeopardy after he suffered a serious wrist injury playing in the New Zealand Open in Auckland. However, he persevered and made one of the great comebacks in New Zealand sports history when, three years following the injury, he won the Johnnie Walker Classic in Taiwan.

Cushla McGillivray
Christchurch

After representing Taranaki in hockey, Cushla McGillivray (née Sullivan) moved to Christchurch where throughout the 1960s and 70s she was one of the best golfers in the country. Representing Canterbury she won multiple New Zealand and inter-provincial titles. She represented New Zealand at the prestigious Espirito Santo tournament in Madrid, Spain and in 1974 she won the New Zealand Women's Match Play title.

But at one stage in her career she was suspended from playing for three months by the New Zealand Women's Golf Association when her name appeared in a Christchurch newspaper advertisement for sporting apparel. Though she was never paid any money for the use of her name, just the suggestion of a commercial endorsement was enough for golf authorities to declare it a violation of her amateur status.

Today, McGillivray is a member of the Clearwater Resort Golf Club where she plays off a 7 handicap and, with that, is a senior Canterbury representative. Also active in bowls, she was most recently the convenor of the New Zealand junior women's bowls selection panel and is a member of the organising committee for the 2008 World Bowls Championship to be held in Christchurch. She retired after nearly 20 years as the executive director of the Canterbury Law Society.